Naming Your Teeth

Even More Observations from a Working Poet

D1564451

Poets notice what other people miss.
Nationally-known poet Molly Fisk's singular
perspective on love, death, grammar, lingerie,
small towns, and the natural world
will get you laughing, crying, and thinking.

Naming Your Teeth

Even More Observations from a Working Poet

Molly Fisk

Story Street Press
Nevada City, California
2018

Published by Story Street Press
10068 Newtown Rd.
Nevada City, CA 95959
e-mail: molly@mollyfisk.com
www.mollyfisk.com

This edition was produced for on-demand distribution by
ingramspark.com and createspace.com for Story Street Press.

Cover design: Maxima Kahn
Cover photo: Jutta Kirchner
Cover tiger: Ina, born in Vienna on June 24, 2008
Back cover photo: Smit Patel on Unsplash
Author photo: Aeron Miller Photography
Typesetting: Wordsworth/Laurence Brauer
Technical Support: Charlotte Peterson, Paul Emery
Financial Support: 61 wonderful patrons (see page 169)
Original inspiration: Carolyn Crane
Frequency: KVMR 89.5 FM Nevada City, CA (105.1 Truckee,
104.7 Woodland, 88.3 Placerville, kvmr.org), The California
Report, KQED 88.5 FM San Francisco, CA (89.3 Sacramento)
In some instances, names have been changed to protect the
innocent. Most of the time they remain intact to celebrate
and encourage the guilty.

Printed in the United States of America

ISBN: 978-0-9894958-8-2

Dedicated to my two godsons, Kristofer & Pascal

and their two brothers, Nicholas & Gabriel

Also by Molly Fisk

poems:

The More Difficult Beauty
Listening to Winter
Terrain (co-author)
Salt Water Poems

essays/radio commentary:

Houston, We Have a Possum
Using Your Turn Signal Promotes World Peace
Blow-Drying a Chicken

Contents

I

II

III

IV

V

I

How to Avoid a Boring Life

It is a truth universally acknowledged in our part of the county that the absolutely best view is to be found while waiting in line at the dump. Three or four cars back, you can see miles of the Sierra Nevada stretching south toward Yosemite. This is where you realize it's already snowed up there, or it hasn't. This is where you think of taking photos but then have to pull forward so they can assess how much you're getting rid of and therefore how much to charge you. Which, in my case yesterday, was nothing, because the broken patio umbrella and 33-year-old ironing board could be classified as metal and taken to a secret location where leaving them off was free.

I am never sorry when things turn out to be free, even though I was armed with small bills. And I'm always happy to be directed to secret locations, since much of the time I try to live my life as if I were a Russian spy only masquerading as a middle-aged American poet.

You should try this. Whenever you feel life has gotten unbearably boring, just imagine you aren't really yourself, but a notorious Russian spy pretending to work in the IT Department of AJA Video or as the produce manager of Safeway and your day will get immediately more interesting. How, for instance, and when are you communicating with your handlers in the mother country? Is it by two-way wrist radio like Dick Tracy in the 1950s or with your cell phone? What kind of information are you supposed to gather? Maybe it's not enough to memorize everyone's order as you pull shots at Starbucks, and you have to time the Thursday meetings of X and Y and note which table they sit at so you can set up your secret camera. Maybe if someone orders a Chai frappucino macciato al dente with no foam that's the signal for you to say "Venti or grande? Twenty-two minutes on table 5, thank you for your order, that'll be $9.50 at the window!" I mean there could be a vast network of former USSR spooks who never came in from the cold! It's very exciting, and can vastly improve a day at work if you do it right.

I picked that ironing board up off the streets
of Cambridge, Mass. on trash night in 1982, by
the way, and it gave me very good service until
recently when it stopped opening. The metal whatsis
underneath just wouldn't budge. Since I iron about
every three years, I figured I shouldn't keep it
around to clutter up the house.

This is why I was waiting in line at the dump
looking at that amazing view, and why I think it's
inevitable the dump will some day close and be
made into condominiums. It had nothing to do with
telling the metal collection department in their
secret location that Ilya Kuryakin is landing at our
municipal airport this afternoon in a Cessna 172
with green stripes. Which you did not hear from me,
I'm just an ordinary poet and life coach.

This message will self-destruct in 60 seconds.

Renting a Wife

Long, long ago, I think it was the 1980s, a business appeared on the radar called Rent-a-Wife. It did not involve, let me say at once, prostitution. Not that kind of rent and not that kind of wife.

As I recall it was started in Seattle by a couple of women who saw a niche. For a reasonable sum per hour, they'd pick up your dry cleaning, wait for the plumber, return videos and library books, maybe do a little grocery shopping. I don't think cooking or cleaning were part of the bargain — that niche being already filled by chefs, house cleaners, and maids. Likewise, they didn't do yard work. The concept was merely racing around town running errands a working person probably couldn't leave the office long enough to do, like getting your tires rotated.

Many of us second-wave feminists felt mixed about this business model. On the one hand, we scoffed at the name, with its sexist slant and

assumptions about what wives did with their time.
"Good grief," we muttered to each other. "Really?
In 1985!?" Everyone we knew, male and female, was
working, and small-size entrepreneurial ventures
hadn't really become a thing yet, nor the now-
ubiquitous home office, so the tradition of a person
staying home all day was not part of our world. Back
then people didn't tend to marry right out of college,
if they went to college, so no one had actual wives or
husbands yet, either, nor kids to be looked after.

On the other hand, it being the '80s, a lot of
us had dry cleaning. (It was not a decade of wash-
and-wear, you'll remember: women wore suits with
huge shoulder pads.) Many of us wished there were
someone around to go get the oil changed (if you
lived in California), or pick up dinner (if you lived
in Chicago). Another body to help with life's many
chores sounded heavenly.

I checked on Google this morning, and there
are still outfits called Rent-a-Wife providing these
services. I didn't click on the one in Thailand.
You can also Rent-a-Husband, if you need a drain
unstopped or anything else on your so-called "honey
do" list. Try not to let that soft porn plot begin to
unspool in your head...I mean it. Turn your mind
to outrage instead. People still think women can't

unstop their own drains? Really? In 2018? There is also Rent-a-Spouse, which sounds more promising, but the jobs are divided strictly along gender lines.

The world is a very strange place and full of surprises., especially on Google. Today, you can apparently rent a mom or dad to stand in at your wedding. You can rent good-looking fake friends to populate your Instagram photos. Cats, dogs, expensive cars, cockatiels, even grandchildren are available to boost your social media image.

I can't tell if this is hilarious or just incredibly sad, or both.

Probably both.

The punchline, though, goes back to the mid-'80s, because — maybe you saw this coming — far and away the majority of people who rented wives were, of course, women.

Ecstasy & Laundry

In my many years of curiosity and nosiness,
I've never studied Buddhism. I have many friends
who do, and a certain amount of the vocabulary
and attitude of this religion — as practiced by
well-meaning North Americans — has filtered into
my consciousness. Which I guess is why the phrase
"after the ecstasy, the laundry" ran through my
mind when I was folding towels just now. It's the
title of a book by Jack Kornfield I've never read,
although I mean to.

After the Ecstasy, the Laundry. It's such a good
description to me of the ups and downs of life. A
rueful, ironic, but forgiving tone, saying we're-all-
in-this-mess-together, encouraging us not to put on
airs because inevitably we'll be brought down to
earth in the end. I sometimes wonder why there's
so much laundry in relation to ecstasy — around
here it's often "after the laundry, how about a little

more laundry" — but I don't mean to complain.
Ecstasy, when it comes along, is far more memorable
than hauling the green basket full of discount-Ralph
Lauren sheets from Ross that I've had for eight
years now up to my washer and dryer in the garage.
It really does balance out. Or at least I think it does.
The last ecstatic moment I had escapes me, to tell
you the truth.

It wasn't romantic or sexual, I know that much.
It didn't have to do with literary glory or financial
windfalls, because those are rarer than hen's teeth
around here, as my grandmother used to say. It was
probably one of two things. Either I wrote a poem
that I really liked, and felt that electric moment
afterward of intense satisfaction and rightness. Or
else it had something to do with birds.

Seeing a mountain bluebird on the wire out my
bathroom window while I brush my teeth has often
given me an intense rush of joy. The haunting calls
of sandhill cranes overhead as they migrate north
can do it. Or the sight of two thousand tundra swans
settling into Marysville's flooded rice fields, making
their unholy racket.

If there is a heaven, my grandmother is up there
wondering how on earth I, an avian ignoramus as
far as she was concerned, developed this thing about

birds. It puzzles me, too: I didn't see it coming,
it's just unfolded incrementally over the years.
Something about the aliveness and alertness of
birds, their quickness of motion or in the case of
pelicans, their prehistoric dignity, just thrills me.
How they're strange and unknowable, yet beautiful,
and all around us. They fit perfectly into the slot in
my head that doesn't want to call anything "God"
but is looking for a metaphor for grace, and Spirit,
and the Buddhist's lovingkindness.

   I'm afraid this is what happens when you get
sassy and start to call yourself a lapsed Unitarian.
God comes and finds you, in one of His (or Her)
many disguises, and just to prove He can do it,
lapse or no lapse, tricks you into recognizing Him in
the shadow of a great blue heron lifting over a salt
marsh at dusk.

One of the Seven Billion

It's hopelessly old-fashioned, but I'm having
the best time reading a book. It's called *The Book of
Joy*, a title I would have ridiculed back in the day.
"Joy, schmoy!" I can hear myself grumbling, passing
a bookstore window display in Chicago or Boston.
I was very smart back then, cynical, unmoved by
anything I thought was sappy. I had no idea how
much emotional pain I carried around, how much
contempt for everything. *Argh*. I can barely stand
to think about it. That poor woman! And my poor
friends who had to put up with me!

Luckily, my life fell apart. There's nothing
more useful for opening your heart than a great
big disaster, as long as you can manage to live
through it. I'll tell you that story another time.
For now, believe me: I was proud, entitled, smug,
righteous, all that sorry stuff. If I experienced joy,
I don't remember those moments. All I remember

is low-grade dissatisfaction that seemed to have no source.

The Book of Joy relays a week-long conversation between His Holiness the Dalai Lama and Archbishop Desmond Tutu. They discuss, of course, joy, its characteristics, how to find it, the obstacles to feeling it and how to practice overcoming them. All of this is interesting information, much of which I'd heard before. What's best about the book is that it's completely hilarious. These venerable codgers, both in their 80s now, are like well-matched tennis stars lobbing incredible shots back and forth and cracking each other up between sets. Tutu envies those huge stadium audiences HH can draw, and thinks the Tibetan goes on too long when answering questions. As they rag on each other like brothers — about food, Heaven and Hell, and how early each one gets up in the morning — the love shines through.

What a relief for them both to have a friend who doesn't idolize them, to have a peer! They're each so important to their followers and to the world. Even though they emphasize being ordinary — just one of the seven billion, the Dalai Lama likes to say — their influence is so vast it's hard for the ordinariness to peek through. This story opens that window a little wider for the rest of us, and spreads the joy of their friendship out into the world.

Half-way into the book it's clear that joy comes via human connection and is strengthened by feeling suffering head-on and then letting it go. Simple concepts, nowhere near easy to do. Tutu says over and over not to blame ourselves, that humans are frail. I think of the hardships they've been through, the death threats they currently live under, and am amazed at their resilience even though I've felt it myself: that little wellspring of joy despite everything bad going on around me. The strange receding of chaos into a moment that's pure and unexpected, and just as real as the dreadfulness.

I'm not grateful for my own suffering — that would be more enlightenment than I can currently muster. And I don't wish disasters on you. But if one *should* ever arise, I hope it helps to know that as well as being completely horrible, it's also a short-cut to joy.

Or Etcetera

I am, once again, in a coffee shop. The bakers
and prep cooks in the back are banging pots and
pans around and discussing how long it will take
to get to Mars: general consensus, six months.
Meanwhile, a Doors song is on the radio, one that
came out when I was in the 8th grade.

This is how weird life is: people chopping oyster
mushrooms to a tune written before they were
born. I wonder if anyone thought about Beethoven's
Moonlight Sonata this way: "Sheesh, why are they
still playing that old thing 50 years later?!? Isn't
there any *new* music?"

Someone back there has looked up the Mars trip
and discovered it takes 300 days. I love overhearing
their conversations. I think the instant-information
age might be quietly ruining our sense of wonder,
though, in both definitions of the word — the
questioning one and the awestruck, amazed one.

Finding answers so quickly has got to do damage to human resilience.

I did not mean to get philosophical and depressing this early in the morning! It's a sunny day, too warm for February but still incredibly enjoyable, and I don't mean to bum you out. I'm also just as addicted to fast information as the next person, so I'm not trying to sound holier-than-thou. But what poets do, and all writers, and most artists, even Jim Morrison and Ludwig von Beethoven, is to notice things, and I am noticing. After that, we make connections, ask questions that usually don't have obvious answers or maybe any answers at all, and then write, paint, dance, sing, or etcetera how we feel about it.

So I'm just doing my job here in this popular café in the Sierra foothills of Northern California, USA, in the early 21-first century, for better or worse. Many of us around the globe are wondering what will happen next, and when. It looks like spring is a month early in my town. Will the almond trees all blossom and then a March frost ruin the crop? Will we stop having winters and just slide from October over into April? There are probably forecast models to look up, but they are guesses: no one really knows.

Living with uncertainty like this requires a kind of alertness that most people aren't used to, and it's both refreshing and nerve-wracking. In a way, for the so-called "first world," it's like what my friends with experience have told me about being poor: not knowing if you'll have enough of whatever you're going to need to be okay, not knowing what to do about it, and having to live in that tension. Given this analogy, the people who are already accustomed to so much tension are going to be better at coping than the rest of us.

Now the Doobie Brothers are wafting out from the kitchen on the scent of frying onions. I can't believe, if you want to know the truth, that I've lived this long.

I hope whatever happens, there will still be some kind of music, although it would be fine with me if it weren't exclusively from 1971.

Boomer Childlessness

Maybe because I never had kids, I'm fascinated by the lives of families. I observe them out in the world, hear about them from friends, and as I sit quietly in my house of one — usually on the sofa with a couple of cats trying to balance on my lap at the same time — I wonder about the pros and cons of being a parent.

I asked someone recently, after her child's birthday, what it was like having a six-year-old. She took a drink of her iced tea, and said: "It's kind like having your own personal house fly." I didn't spit my own iced tea onto the café's white table cloth, but it was a near thing. "*What?!?!*" I said.

"She's wonderful, don't get me wrong, but every 30 seconds she comes over to ask me another un-related question, and by lunch I'm a complete wreck."

I've met this child, she's great. I love the phase when you can see kids start learning to think, to

make sense of language and the world around them.
But I never spend more than an hour at a time
with one, and often their parents are around. Three
weeks of questions would have me robbing a bank
so I could hire a nanny or afford to send them to
boarding school.

I've seen many phases of child-rearing, from
pregnancy and newborns to great grandchildren.
I've watched adoptions, fostering, only children,
great big families, blended step-households, and
orphans. I always imagined, without thinking much
about it, that I'd have kids of my own. But when the
relevant years were passing, my attention was on
my own survival and I missed the boat. I also didn't
want to raise a kid alone because I was so angry — I
didn't think I'd be a good risk without someone else
in the house to steady me.

I've had a pretty good life without them, including
the love of a fabulous niece and lots of fun with other
people's children. Now that I'm in my 60s, there's
talk about what will happen to Baby Boomers with no
families to take care of them at the end of life. This
is a bit crazy-making, reinforcing the cultural myth
that we should have had children in the first place.
Now we're going to be shown up again as outcasts by
having to pay strangers to change our adult diapers.

My friend Ellen has asked her three kids to push her off a steep hiking trail in the Rockies when the time comes, and says she's sure they'd be happy to do that for me, too. Volunteering one's progeny for manslaughter is a sign of a true friend, but I have my doubts... I don't even think they're going to do it for her. And *getting* to the hiking trail might be a problem.

I'll have to think about this aspect of child-lessness and get back to you. You can't really plan to trip over a cat at the salient moment. Cats are notoriously unreliable.

Naming Your Teeth

A three-year-old I know just explained to his
mom that he needed an umbrella because it was
hot in the yard and "there isn't a shade structure."
Coffee almost flew out my nose when she told
me this, I was laughing so hard. The wonders of
language and watching people learn it make me
incredibly happy. Also, the way children sponge
up whatever they hear around them. And how
inventive and fun they can be before they've picked
up most of the rules. Plus, when did we come to this
goofy stage of modern life where we adults invent
generic technical terms like "shade structure?"
Good grief. Though if he'd said "there isn't a
pergola" I probably would have fainted.

One of the vast irritations about getting older
is discovering that the stupid clichés we've been
hearing all our lives are actually true. Kids *do* say
the darnedest things and youth *is* wasted on the

young. It's so annoying. Maybe not as annoying as being dead and unable to have an opinion, but still, *very* annoying.

Just as I liked watching my friends have kids, now I like seeing them with their grandchildren. They are totally besotted, which is another true cliché, and it's a fact that skipping the middle generation eases a lot of friction. One of my friends has taught her grandson to identify birds by their calls. Another gives her's home-made ice cream lessons. I, as the grandparents' friend and a writer, am often in charge of language: I show kids how to look up the roots of words and throw in a grammar rule or two while I'm at it. I teach them satisfying new swear words like "flummox" and "gewurtztraminer." And they clue me in on strange modern inventions, such as "fleek."

The business about the shade structure is excellent, but in honor of two additional all-too-accurate clichés: "out of the mouths of babes," and "the road to hell is paved with good intentions," my favorite story comes from the brother of one of my godsons.

Nicholas is kind of my godson, too, by proxy, but a few years younger. One day I was walking him down the driveway to the car — I think he was

about five. At the time I didn't realize that some
kids don't develop a sense of humor right away,
it can take a few years for this part of their brain
to get organized. Just to be friendly, thinking a
godmother ought to make some sort of an effort,
but feeling a little awkward and therefore trying to
be amusing, I asked Nick if he'd named all his teeth
yet.

He turned his head to look up at me with the
clearest expression in his eyes — an equal blend
of surprise, disbelief, scorn, and pity — and said,
forcefully, enunciating every syllable in case my
hearing was as bad as my comprehension:

"*All* of my teeth are named Nicholas!"

#14

It's 6 a.m. It's dark. I'm still in my nightgown, but I've brushed my teeth, which I do before everything else. I can't stand that feeling of having little sweaters on my teeth, as a friend likes to describe it. One of these teeth, #14, which is on the top left, second from the end, I've just brushed for the last time. At noon today, it's coming out. The bone around its roots is disintegrating, apparently, and if they cut it off at the gum-line and put a special membrane across the cut, the bone may grow back, which would be a good thing for #13 and #15, as well as my jaw.

To look at me, here on the couch in front of the fire, writing in a notebook, you wouldn't think I was in hysterics. But I am. My own special kind, which is so muted no one but me can see it.

My periodontist is a cheerful guy, immensely capable and kind, who likes poetry. If anyone's going to take out #14, I want him to do it. But when he told me, cheerfully, that it had to come out, I nearly lost my lunch. He thinks #30 will have to come out too, because it's so loose. I'm thinking of using Gorilla Glue to keep it in place and not telling him.

After I left his office I burst into tears. Who knew I was so attached to a tooth? But of course, it's not just the tooth, per se, it's what the tooth represents. First of all, it's *my* tooth, and I don't want to lose anything that's mine — I want to be intact. Second, it opens that creaking door to old age and death. First a tooth, then pretty soon I won't be able to drive at night or walk into town on my own two feet. Rest homes and feeding tubes are sure to follow.

As I drove home, I thought about all the cancer patients I teach, half of whom have had mastectomies, and how clueless I've been, nodding sagely when they described their feelings. How did they learn to bear it? If I'm this distraught over one tooth, how can I look them in the eye at our next class, much less have the gall to offer them solace?

I felt the swirl of emotions that arises when something bad happens: *Oh, no! Could I have* caused *this? Why is this happening to me? I haven't done anything wrong! This isn't fair! How will I ever stand it? I* can't *stand it.* All the stages of grief passed through my head, including bargaining: *I promise I'll floss three times a day if you'll just let me keep this tooth.*

Maybe if I'd flossed three times a day, #14 would not be in this fix, but I didn't. I just can't do all the things I'm supposed to do. And maybe nothing would have helped these Anglo-Saxon teeth, which have crumbled in the mouths of my forebears for centuries.

The sky is getting light now, and I have to get going. I'm giving #14 what she wants for breakfast, her last meal: scrambled eggs with mushrooms and parmesan. I'm grateful she's been with me all these years. Once she's out, I'm bringing her home for a burial under the sour cherry tree, next to Max, Seamus, and Red Jack, my beloved cats.

Pinball

I think I always expected my life to be like a
movie. With a plot that made sense, recognizable
characters, and of course a happy ending. I don't
know where I got this idea. It sure turns out to be
wrong, or else I landed in one of those films by Luis
Buñuel.

For one thing, there's either too much going on
or not enough. What movie would bounce its main
character from job to unrelated job like this? Waitress,
hotel maid, flunky in an engineering firm, sales clerk,
sweater designer, banker, bookkeeper, small business
consultant, contract investigator for the EEOC,
poetry teacher, editor, and now — just for a lark —
advertising copy writer? After all that action, what
screenplay would require the heroine to eat dinner by
herself on the same green sofa for years on end?

The plot is not clear to me at all and, while
I love the characters myself, they aren't exactly

recognizable — they're much too complicated to be *just* the kindly neighbor or the faithful boyfriend. I've had eight boyfriends, not all of them precisely faithful, and none of my neighbors has been "kindly" in that unctuous movie way. Human, yes. Kindly, no.

Instead of a movie, my life has turned out to be a pinball game: lots of tension, short bursts of excitement, some shouting, long stretches of the doldrums, followed by banging on the side of the machine, renewed energy, and another try at manipulating the ball into the right place so the bell will ring. It feels extremely random and fragmented, not to mention repetitious.

I'm thinking about this today because I just saw a Bullock's oriole drink some of last night's rainwater from a leaf on my apple tree. My heart raced, but I stood incredibly still so as not to scare him off. I wanted to moan and *leap* with delight, he was so beautiful.

This is what saves me from whichever stage the pinball game is in: something completely real and amazing. Does this happen to you? Sometimes the light as it pours out of clouds over our local grocery store will stop me in my tracks. Once in a while it's the color of my seven-year-old friend Dashiell's cheek. Or a hug from somebody with arms long enough to go all the way around me. The taste of a really good grapefruit.

It's handy that once you know what works to get you out of trouble, you can practice the technique. After I learned to recognize those astonishing moments, I began to look for them. To walk slowly enough across the grocery store parking lot that I'd notice if any light was pouring through the clouds. To stand still long enough to be hugged, and not pull away. Even to go to the movies when something looked like a good bet, which is, in my case, not Buñuel but anything with Chris Cooper or Yves Montand.

I hope your life is a bowl of cherries or a cabaret, my friend. Or a movie with a happy ending. But I have a feeling I'm about to hear "Tilt!" again, any minute now.

Maybe I'll get lucky and see a Scarlet tanager first.

Appreciation 101

As you know, I'm not just a poet, I'm also a life coach. I can hear your inhalation before you let out a huge groan, but swallow that sound, the kind of coaching I do is pretty radical. Yes, I can help you figure out how to clean your garage, apply to college, finish your novel, or ask for a divorce. But I'm also going to be teaching you, over and over, how much our culture has influenced your thinking and how many of its unhelpful messages we've all absorbed.

One of the biggest we get hammered with — in advertising, work, school, and the rest of our waking hours — is the idea of "false scarcity." There isn't enough, or soon there won't be enough, and this will put us in danger. Whether it's a run on organic eggs at Grocery Outlet or a rush to buy Boeing shares when the price dips, we've been trained to respond to threats of scarcity.

Much of American life has been built on the
concept, since it's such a good way to make people
go shopping, and we're in a capitalist economy. But
really, how many eggs can your ice box hold, and how
long do eggs last, anyway? If you can take a minute
to stand still, often your common sense will appear to
remind you there is not currently an egg shortage in
California. Maybe there will be some day, but there
isn't one today. And today is actually where we are.

I mention this because false scarcity leaks
from economic terrain to pollute our brains in
other regions, including the lobe of appreciation.
People used to think hearing compliments would
go to a child's head and she'd become stuck-up or
egotistical, so doled them out sparingly.

This is ridiculous. Praise doesn't make you
stuck-up, it makes you feel warm, and known,
and loved. Who doesn't want some of that? Yet we
regularly don't say the sweet things we're thinking
about friends and colleagues, strangers, even the
cashiers at Grocery Outlet. This is false scarcity
in action. Appreciation is free, it's beneficial to
the recipient, it makes the donor feel better, and
it's a way to tell the truth, something we all could
emphasize in this modern world full of spin and
fear-mongering.

Because we aren't used to it, though, we have to practice — it can feel awkward. When you start, keep it short and simple. "How nice of you to help me take my bags out to the car!" "Thanks for holding the door, stopping the bus, letting me go ahead of you in line with my carton of milk." If someone's smile just made your day, tell them! If you appreciate your kid being ready for school in the morning, your spouse getting home on time for dinner, your dog not chasing the cat, say so. There is no limit, here.

You're allowed to tell people good things more than twice a century. Try twice a day, to begin with, and then ramp it up.

II

Backing In

While all of you were busy sleeping, working,
or eating a late lunch, I have been out in the wider
world conducting important research. You've probably
noticed that in the last, oh, three months, people
have begun to park backwards in Nevada County
parking spaces. It's very weird. I'm here to report
that this trend is also popular all over Massachusetts.
In airport lots, churches, even the famous Clam Box
restaurant in Ipswich, at least one car is in the James
Bond position, primed for a speedy getaway.

I have no idea what's going on here, and living
in a rural backwater it may already have peaked
as an urban trend and I'm just finding out about it
now. But it's quite noticeable, once you notice it —
kind of like everyone dying their hair turquoise blue,
or wearing Crocs all of a sudden.

This morning, I buttonholed (now there's a
great old-fashioned word!) someone after watching

him back into a spot at a café. In his case, he said, he'd ripped the front bumper off his Porsche one too many times on the cement barrier that so many parking spaces feature. Neither of us could think of the name for the cement barrier, if there is one. "But," he said, "the reason I've heard it's good to back in is that you're more alert when you park than when you leave, since you've been driving already to get wherever you're parking, and therefore you should do the hard part then. After your lunch or beer or whatever, it's safer to just roll forward and be on your way."

I am thinking it may be easier to back up in a Porsche than my 16-year-old Highlander, but I don't have personal experience, and asking him if I could try it this morning seemed a bit crass. I don't think either of us had had enough coffee for that kind of negotiation. For me, backing out will always be easier because the lane behind me is big, whereas the parking place is small. Backing in, you have to be careful not to whack the adjacent cars, of course, and also you have to judge the amount of room for door opening, in my case a crucial factor. I've stood around in quite a few parking lots waiting for the return of oblivious thin people who parked so close to my door that I couldn't sidle in and open it.

So despite the raised eyebrow of my inner James
Bond (played by Sean Connery and don't tell me
how sexist he is, I already know it. You can't control
your inner life's casting decisions.), I won't be
adopting this habit. I'd like to know what started it,
though. Is some sexy TV surgeon or district attorney
backing into parking spots all the time? Are
unconscious fears brought on by national politics
fueling (ahem) the trend?

The People's Republic

I'm sitting at a small metal table outside a cafe in Berkeley, California watching the world go by. So many bicycles! And men wearing hats. Not baseball caps, but real hats, and they aren't young men, either. Fire trucks, garbage trucks, the kind of city busses that wheeze. I'm on a corner with a four-way stop, so I get to see what everyone thinks a stop really is, and let me tell you, opinions vary!

A few kids with their moms or dads, but not enough to indicate a school nearby. Beside me on the street is one of those rent-a-bike stands with 17 receptacles, 10 of which are empty. There's a kiosk attached, where you pay, and then, as I understand it, you can ride around town and drop the bike off somewhere else, at another stand. If you were to squint, and also imagine yourself up in the foothills where I live at the beginning of the last century, you might see horses tied to a railing in exactly this posture.

A person drinking coffee at a sidewalk cafe with wicker chairs like this could also indulge in a fantasy of being in Paris, an ex-pat like Gertrude Stein, but then a boombox goes by, and the sight of someone's rear-end encased in turquoise lycra dispels the illusion. Some of the cyclists are wearing tie-dye, though, and are more my age than not, which is heartening to see. They are usually female, riding in pairs while not stopping at the stop sign, and deep in shouted conversation.

I'm in the shade wearing a sweater, but many other people have on those new down jackets with very narrow horizontal poofinesses — what is the word for that? Channels, maybe. The places on a down garment where there are no seams. And the jackets, so far, are all black. I've probably seen 35 of them in the last hour. What this means, I cannot tell you, but we could make up a reason: Black is the color of city life, being both sophisticated and anonymous, for instance. Or people in Berkeley are always cold due to looking toward the Pacific — their body temperature responds to the metaphor of endless chilly water and uncharted depths.

Even when we don't think so, humans are constantly making up stories and reasons to fill in what we don't already know. We speculate, and unless we find out accurate information, those speculations, originally wispy and light, begin to thicken into certainty. This is why — oh, darn it, I guess I'm heading for a moral, which I didn't mean to do — one should keep an eye out, and not believe everything you think. I should, anyway — I can't speak for anyone else. You, my dears, are on your own.

There are wider applications than Berkeley outerwear that we could bring into the discussion here, of course, but let's not. It's a beautiful morning and I'm almost done with my coffee. Suffice it to say that I'm waving from this rickety table on College Avenue, fellow human, sending you love and wishing you the best of luck with speculation management!

The Dark Ale Experiment

Is a person drinking beer at 8 a.m. all that
different from a person drinking coffee? I'm
watching someone at my local café's counter
consume a huge tumbler of dark ale along with a
nourishing organic breakfast, and my mind is going
wild with judgement and worry.

Humans (of whom I am one) are so fond of
stories, of making random observations into a
coherent whole. Whether or not this amalgamation
is *true* doesn't seem to matter much, it's just
distressing for the human brain to notice isolated
bits and pieces and leave them alone.

As with many things, distress stems from a
feeling of being unsafe. If we can see that — for
example — a white stretch limo parked outside a
local restaurant is connected to something, perhaps
it's prom night or they're making a movie in the
next town, our brains relax and go back to our own

concerns. The anomaly makes sense, and if we don't have a kid at prom or care about the movie, it's really none of our business.

This middle-aged man in the Guatemalan shirt drinking ale is none of my business either, *ahem*, but as someone who needed to and did stop drinking a few decades ago, I'm afraid watching anyone drink beer before noon feels like a siren inside my head: shocking and dangerous. So I have to work a bit more to soothe my nervous system and let go of my judgements.

My life coach — don't you have a life coach? They're so useful, everyone should have a life coach — says that since we're making up a story anyway, we might as well make it up to our own advantage. Think about the ramifications of *that* for a moment... Therefore, I've decided this gentleman is a scientist working on the effects of dark ale on the human body at different times of day. He's doing his own research before the 500-person experiment at U.C. Davis begins next month, and this is the 8 a.m. ale-ingestion day. Tomorrow it will be 9:30, the next day 11, and on by 90-minute increments through all 24 hours. There are of course many factors involved in the experiment that he can't control for as a single participant observing himself, but it's a responsible act to first do anything you're going to ask other people to do, and he is a trained professional, not the alcoholic I was worrying he might be.

I don't use the word *alcoholic*, actually, because it's up to the individual to name themselves one way or the other. Speaking strictly from my side of the fence, what I can truly say is only that someone's drinking (or drug use, or overeating, or whatever addiction it is) bothers me. Or doesn't bother me.

Now it's 8:30. My scientist has drained his glass and is getting up to go. I'm feeling much calmer now, and sort of fond of the guy. What do you think, should the 500 subjects all wear Guatemalan shirts as part of the experiment, or is that a random and unrelated matter?

Dead Canary

I don't drink beer, but I'm sitting at a restaurant counter in front of the list of their beer offerings, brewed in-house as is the trend right now. When I did drink beer, it was Rolling Rock or Dos Equis in long-necked bottles. Massachusetts in the 1980s.

This beer has names referring to our river's favorite swimming holes: Mother's Beach Blonde and Emerald Pool IPA. I like these better than a nearby brewery's: Dead Canary. Why would you be moved to drink this? People are very strange, it turns out. The name might derive from our history as a mining center and the tradition of lowering caged canaries into mine shafts before the people went down, to make sure the air was breathable. Which doesn't improve the allure, animal sacrifice being less appetizing than mere bird cadavers, at least in my house.

Bob Hass, former Poet Laureate of these United States, once wrote: "Of all the laws that bind us to the past, the names of things are stubbornest." This hit me in the solar plexus, so I taped it to my computer monitor. On my deathbed, may that not be soon, I'll probably remember there was a beer named Dead Canary and forget the names of all my lovers and my cats.

It's easy to make fun of things you don't know much about, but I'm trying to cure myself of the tendency to scoff and ridicule. It's just not a good look on any of us, not to mention far too close to the behavior of certain national politicians whom no one wishes to emulate. Therefore I won't elaborate, as I am tempted to do, on this sign's descriptions of the beers, calling them "fruity, with hints of coffee, clean, complex, and containing tropical citrus notes." And "dry roasted," which sounds like they're describing nuts. And even "dry." What does that actually mean? Just like white wine, beer has always seemed to me irredeemably wet. I don't know what "hoppy" tastes like, but it makes sense since beer is made from hops and I've seen those growing in a field beside Interstate 80.

These beers have won four California State Fair ribbons, so people clearly admire them, and the restaurant is always packed at Happy Hour, another endorsement.

Beer is not my bailiwick, but language certainly is, so now I'm wondering why the containers one can buy in which to take beer home are called "growlers." Bears, dogs, even tigers growl. No one here seems to know how beer got in on the act, so I must turn to Brewmaster Google, who says:

The term likely dates from the late 19th century when fresh beer was carried from the local pub to one's home by means of a small galvanized pail. It is claimed the sound that the carbon dioxide made when it escaped from the lid as the beer sloshed around sounded like a growl.

I can see it now: I'll be sitting on some floral couch in a distant future, cheerful and dotty, smiling up at people I love whose names I can't remember and repeating like a boozy pirate or someone's badly trained mynah bird:

"Growler!" "Hoppy, hoppy!" "Give me that Dead Canary!"

50 Labor in Vain Rd.

When people are 88 years old, it is prudent,
even sensible, to imagine that they might die fairly
soon. And still, we didn't, no one expected, I wasn't
ready, and my Aunt Mary's death brings back the
other deaths I'm not ready for that have already
happened. My mother's, 18 years ago. My father's:
34. Some part of me still paused there, like an actor
in a film clip mid-gesture after you've hit the remote
to go get a glass of water or see who's at the door.

I've sat on my couch here in California for half
an hour trying to formulate a next sentence, and
it isn't happening. It's way too soon to be coherent
about what Mary meant to me. So I'm going to
ramble and ask your forgiveness.

One of her seven grandsons posted on Instagram
a photo of a can of beer balanced on the yellow soap
dish in her upstairs shower. You know those old-
fashioned ceramic units that fit into the tiled wall:

a corrugated soap dish with a mysterious bar across
the top? He'd parked an IPA there, perfect fit, and
used the hashtag #showerbeer, which makes me
wonder for his health but maybe it's a thing among
young men these days, I don't know. He wrote some
words about spending time in and out of that house
— first Mary and John's house, then Mary and
Bob's, and then for two years only Mary's.

I understand how he feels about growing up
there — a big old drafty gorgeous New England
farmhouse on a tidal creek. All of us belong to it —
my mother did, my Aunt Net, my siblings, every
grandchild. We slept and ate and played there,
shucked corn, set the table again, rubbed garlic
around the interior and then made dressing in the
big wooden bowl itself and threw the salad stuff
on top. Easy to toss at the table, and no bottles of
dressing to drip — because they always drip — on
the table cloth. The furniture rarely changed in half
a century: a mix of inherited antiques and mid-
60's Scandinavian. White walls, translucent white
curtains, white bookshelves, and big white paper
Japanese lanterns orbiting like moons in every
room.

People often talk about "place" as inspiration.
Even as we looked out the windows, sometimes

lingering, sometimes just in passing, we also saw it
through Mary's eyes in her paintings. The window
sills and salt marsh in every season, every kind of
light. The creek at low tide, the fields in winter.
Mary painted Vermont stone walls and the old brick
riverside buildings of New England mill towns. She
painted pianos and sofas, dining room chairs.

But she laid a permanent claim to the views
from that house in all directions: driveway, shed,
clothesline, fence pickets, angles of porch columns,
marsh grass, willows, the dock, a neighbor's boat at
its mooring, and then the long gaze across Gould's
Creek to the Ipswich River, the edge of Little Neck
and, very faintly, or maybe just in imagination, Plum
Island beyond.

Ipswich Memorial

This weekend I'm traveling back to the landscape of all my childhood summers. I'm going to a funeral, which is sad, though the person who died was 88, which isn't a bad run, and she got to live at home until the end, a great gift her children gave her.

I was named for her, my Aunt Mary, my mother's elder sister. I keep, on my kitchen counter, an old Christmas card she sent me, probably in the 1990s. It's a photograph of one of her paintings, glued to Crane's stationery, and inside her familiar handwriting says what it always said in every Christmas card: Merry Xmas, Molly, much love Mary. First it was Mary & John, and a check for ten dollars I think, probably beginning when I was in high school and buying presents for far-away nieces wasn't high on her list. Her handwriting so much like my mother's, and the "much love," but just a

little sharper, more angular. After college it became
Mary & Bob, and then for the last two years, just
Mary. Later on, somewhere in the middle of my life,
the presents resumed: scarves, books, mittens, once
a blue necklace that I still wear, always wrapped the
same way.

My own niece, Gioia, was laughing about this
when I saw her last month. The Pennington women
wrapped presents in a very specific manner: two or
three sheets of solid-colored tissue paper carefully
folded without any tape and the ribbon holding
it together. No curling the ribbon with scissors,
sometimes not even a bow, just a quick knot. I believe
this is so you can reuse the paper for the next time.
The Pennington girls were a minister's daughters,
born during the Depression, and it still showed.

Mary's survived by my four cousins and their
partners, seven grandsons, one great-grandson. She
lived in the same house for 40 years, so I expect the
memorial, to be held at a church in the center of
town, will overflow with people whose names I've
known all my life and whose faces I won't recognize.
Almost all the parents are gone now. My generation
predominates, gray-haired and seemingly sedate.
I'm interested to find out what the diaspora of those
summers, 1966, '68, '71, looks like.

Belonging seems to be one of the abiding
themes of my life. Where, and to whom, and why,
and then what does that mean, or require, how
does it matter? I got a chance in my thirties when
logic would have taken me away from my family,
but I didn't let go of them. At that point, and since,
belonging outweighs pain. I don't think this is true
for everyone, and I don't know why it's true for me.

I wasn't born when Mary painted the view out a
window in New York that is on this Xmas card, but
I belong to it, too. Seeing the painting on her wall
all my life and its photo here on my counter ties me
to a winter day on East 13th St., and the mystery of
what my not-yet aunt was thinking, something I will
now never be able to ask her.

Nine Short Lives

One of my cats just jumped to the floor from the
bathroom sink, where he'd been sipping drops of
leftover water, and made a very loud thump. I looked
up to see if he was alright. He walked, dignified but
slow, through the door and sat in a patch of sun
to wash his left elbow. It was quite a thorough left
elbow bath, and then, disregarding all other body
parts, he stretched out on the rug and fell asleep.

You know by now that I love cats. I may not
have mentioned, however, that I tend to adopt
families rather than individuals. This one sleeping
here and his sister came to me after an earthquake
in Paso Robles 17 years ago. They'd been found
in a barn, but the earthquake overwhelmed local
shelters with lost pets, so no one could take in feral
kittens. Instead, my friend with the barn drove
them six hours to my house. I'd volunteered to find
homes for them, but in the end I couldn't let them

go. Unusually for rural cats, Sid and Gracie have survived into old age, which is what that thump was about. They're landing harder these days, and sometimes don't complete the upward jumps and end up dangling from the sink's rim by one paw, looking horrified.

Cats are so famously self-sufficient, it's disorienting when they begin to need help. Sid has always been the alpha male, but now Black Jack, only seven, steals his dinner unless I'm around to prevent this. Gracie is constantly cold and even after I've said "no" 46 times and moved her off my lap, I'll look up from a paragraph and find her half on my knee and half on the keyboard.

These events tear at my heartstrings. They're hard to watch in themselves, since I don't want to lose my companions and I get reminded every day that death is coming. None of a cat's nine lives goes much past 20. And they also point to the larger picture of all the aging humans around me. I won't have to build a platform between sink and floor for my cousin Miranda, but at some point she may need my arm when we walk from the car to the movie theater. What's worse is I may need hers.

I've been getting older since mid-July of 1955, but for some reason this year it feels much more noticeable. All my familiars are getting a little grayer or moving slower, forgetting words at a great rate, sometimes neglecting to wash their right elbows. I still feel about 32, only happier and wiser, but don't ask me to race you across the street. I'm not sure my knees or boobs can take it.

Maybe there's a symbiotic reason we fall so hard for animals. Maybe it helps to rehearse a few entire life cycles before we're faced with the end of our own. I don't know. Today, I just want everything to stay the same forever, and all of it to be kind, and sweet, and easy.

As younger people like to say: "Yeah, good luck with that."

Let Me Call You Sweetheart

Yesterday a young man called me *sweetheart* and then widened his eyes and asked "Is that OK, to call you *sweetheart*? I call everyone I like *sweetheart*, even the men." To prove this, he raised his voice from behind the counter, aiming at another young man sitting at a nearby table, "Good morning, sweetheart!" The guy grinned, removed his ear buds, and waved at us. I don't believe he had heard a word. This is what it's like right now in my life: people are thinking more about what they're saying and doing, questioning whether habitual responses are valid.

I grew up in a family that hugged a lot, and I just continued the hugging with everyone else automatically. Also, it was the '60s. Then I went through a phase of not wanting to be touched by strangers myself, and suddenly saw, with horror, how unaware my own behavior was. Now, I try to remember to ask people before I touch them, and stay out of range until I get an answer. I sometimes also exaggerate, holding my arms out like a frigate bird's wingspan so no one will mistake that a hug is being offered — an impromptu game of charades.

Have you ever said "no" when someone asked for a hug? It's not that easy. Our culture pressures us in so many ways to go along and not rock the boat. I'm not even talking about instances where desire might be involved.

As an exercise, you could try this. Figure out a phrase you can say and then rehearse a few times — in front of a mirror or with a close person. This is good modeling for kids, too, if you're raising any. "Thanks, but it's a no-hug day for me," or "I'm not taking hugs right now." You can also fib until you've worked up your courage: "Stop! I'm coming down with something!" People are often on auto-pilot, so sometimes I've had to back up or put my hands out in front of me, which is awkward. The whole darn thing is awkward, of course, and it can get worse. Once an acquaintance burst into tears when I stopped her mid-lunge.

But this is clearly about the other person, not about you. In light of current events, it's good to remind ourselves that our bodies belong to us and we're in charge, whether we're a nine-year-old boy wincing as Aunt Ruth tries to pinch our cheek again or a 28-year-old actor not wanting her hope for a movie role to be misconstrued. Also, when you can say *no* to a hug, it makes your *yesses* feel wonderful.

I said to my friend behind the counter, "*Sweetheart* doesn't bother me, but I'm only 62. It can sound disrespectful when you say it to 80-year-olds." He cocked his head and thought for a minute. "It's not quite the right word. You *are* sweet, but you're at least half bad-ass."

I smiled. It's so satisfying to be truly known.

Not Precisely the Right Word

Last week, I went out to lunch with some friends in my fairly groovy rural California town. Many restaurants around here believe in using local produce, and I've noticed this can lead to more specific menu descriptions. It might be the name of the farm: Riverhill, Mountain Bounty, or First Rain. But this time, it was the name of a vegetable: instead of "winter squash ravioli," it was called "Kabocha squash ravioli."

My friends and I are of a certain age, which means that a) we forget things, and b) we don't jump to our phones to look up what we've forgotten. We're of the generation that still likes the meandering conversational process of trying to figure out what the word was. It's part of the fun — perhaps the only fun — of having sieves for brains now. "What was that squash, again? I know it's not *Kombucha*, that's the vinegary drink," said one.

"And it's not *Kubota*, that's the Japanese tractor," said another.

This restaurant uses table cloths and then lays brown kraft paper over them, which is very convenient. I've written six or seven poems on that brown paper over the years. I spelled out *Kombucha* and *Kubota* in maroon ink next to my plate. The waitress came back and we asked her the name of the squash. *K-a-b-o-c-h-a*. Which is, it turns out, Japanese, like the tractor. Then the owner came by and through some mishearing, also a feature of our ages, *Kabuki* and *Kimono* were added to the list, even though they don't end in "a." A certain amount of hilarity ensued, possibly amplified by the Sauvignon Blanc my friends were drinking.

Later in the day I had to run an errand at the nursery, where a different friend works, and while I was buying a saffron-yellow, one-gallon chrysanthemum we passed their big display of pumpkins and squashes, so I told her the story.

"Oh, that's nothing," she said. "You should hear what happens with plant names. One time a very dignified, well-dressed older woman came in here and asked me if I had chlamydia!"

All you gardeners will realize that what the woman meant was *clematis*: a popular variety of climbing vine with gorgeous big flowers, also, coincidentally, of Japanese and Chinese origin. *Chlamydia*, in case you are reaching for your phone to ask Dr. Google, is a fairly unpleasant venereal disease that affects both women and men. The dignified customer was mortified when she figured out what she'd said, of course.

I have no moral for this story: you get to choose your own. Maybe you're thinking it should be "Live fast, die young, and leave a good-looking corpse." Maybe it's a groan of anticipation, like "Get ready for your mind to start embarrassing you in public and make sure you have friends who'll help you laugh about it."

Either way, tip your hat to the eldest around you, who used to be as quick-witted and fleet as the rest of us, unbelievable as that may seem.

Oregon Creek

I'm having the weirdest day. Nothing feels right. This morning, I had a break from my scheduled life and headed east out of town to see fall color in the mountains. Five miles later, I found myself behind an oil tanker truck, and thought, "This isn't going to work." Turned around at the next pull-out and came back. Then I headed south, thinking that at least if I was in an iffy mood I could do some grocery shopping "down the hill." People here sometimes drive an hour to big box stores, and I haven't done that in six months. Only a few minutes later, I realized smoke from all the California fires was thickening around my car, and decided I didn't want to breathe it.

Then I went home, made a pitcher of iced tea, and consulted the cats. Sid and Gracie, my 17-year-olds, were quite clear that I should stay home and sit still please, affording them each half a lap. This

is what they always say, unless a bird has flown into
the house, which is the only thing they'll chase any
more at their advanced ages. Birds pretty much
never fly into our house, however. "I can't stay
home, I'm antsy, I have to GO somewhere!!"

"I'll see you later," I said, and drove north this
time. I dropped a few things at a friend's house even
though she wasn't home, and then kept going, the
road meandering through lots of shade, some lovely
yellow aspens but mostly conifers — dark green
and eighty feet tall. I was still confused, but began
to feel a little more light-hearted and look around.
After half an hour, I crossed the middle fork of our
local, magical river, the Yuba, and saw the sign for a
swimming hole I've sometimes jumped into on hot
days. Unexpectedly, I pulled in and parked.

This is one of those places called a "day use
area," which is the least appealing name for a picnic
spot I have ever heard. Who makes these things
up, anyway, and why did they not hire a poet? Good
grief. A small creek joins the river here and a rope
swing hangs over the bank. I sat listening to the
sound for a while, and then wrote a poem about it,
mentioning God, which is strange, since I'm a lapsed
Unitarian and don't believe in God. He does sneak
into my poems, though, now and again, the rascal.

I got stuck on one word, and made a list of options. What would you call the action of a creek? It's a mix of sound and motion together, and possibly light. *Burbles* was a little too British and maybe archaic. Clatters? Chuckles? Chortles? Churns? Chowders? No, creeks don't *chowder*. Tumbles? Rambles? Scampers? Waddles? Somersaults? Sidles? Sparkles?

Aha. *Sparkles*. I used *sparkles*. It was good with the "k" in *creek* and also in *smoke*, a few lines later.

This is what poets do with our time, in case you were wondering.

III

The Whale Vertebra

When I told my sister I was putting together
another book of radio commentaries, she said:
"You're going to have one about me in there, right?"

I was leaning against my kitchen counter,
resisting the wiles of a cat who thinks dinnertime is
at 11 a.m. She was changing lanes on the Bay Bridge.
Her car has Blue Tooth so somehow phone calls go
through her steering wheel. This terrifies me every
time we talk on the phone. I, the late-adopter, was
holding a landline to my ear with my shoulder.

"I've used all the good ones," I said. "The one
about Fiji, the one about our family not liking
vinegar, and what was...? Oh, that one about your
house burning down."

"Well," she said cheerfully, "I guess you'll have
to write another one, then."

"What, you get to be in every book?!? Since
when?"

NAMING YOUR TEETH 77

"Don't mess with a good thing," she said. "It might be why your books are so popular!"

See what I have to put up with?! I had 14 blissful months as an only child and then *whammo*, this one showed up, born feet first and backward at two in the morning and the party began. Whether I was destined to be the steady-seeming sister, we'll never know, but I took on the role. Sarah wasn't irresponsible exactly, and isn't now, but when she collected a whale's vertebra from a beach in Nova Scotia and left it in a locker at the Boston airport, who had to go collect the darn thing and fly it home to California on United? Exactly. It weighed more than 50 lbs., smelled exactly like the whale it came from, and did not, needless to say, fit into the overhead bin, so I also had to field questions and rude stares as it sat wrapped in brown paper, belted into the seat beside me and the plane filled with the intoxicating aroma of diesel fuel and dead fish. I saw it the other day, on her back porch, 43 years later. I think she uses it as a footstool.

I could go on. *I'm* not friends with Wavy Gravy or Fiji's national rugby team. *I* didn't walk the Pacific Crest Trail before Cheryl Strayed was out of grade school. I've had adventures, don't get me wrong, but Sarah's adventures always seem more

adventurous than anyone else's. This is because she
tells such good stories. It's absurd that I turned out
to be the writer among us.

This week she returned from Paris, where she
spoke at a conference on Applied Improvisation. I'll
let you look that up on your telephone. I told her
to eat a Parisian eclair, which she did right in front
of me, on a video chat thingamajig that she made
me sign up for before she left town. The last thing
I need is an app, for heaven's sake, but I did it: her
enthusiasm brooks no argument. A pistachio eclair.

Paris meant she couldn't go to Burning Man,
but don't worry, she'll be flying to Edmonton soon,
or an elephant preserve in Kenya, or perhaps an
underwater photo excursion off the coast of Bali.

Please pray that there are no oversized
vertebrae involved.

Sea Otters, Bathing

This morning, a friend and I spend some time standing at the edge of a small bay, watching two sea otters give themselves baths. I had no idea that an animal who lives in water would need a bath, much less one full of salt. These guys were very good at washing; they clearly had practiced. But they also regularly lost their balance and slipped under the surface — sometimes lengthwise, tipping sideways the way you roll a kayak, and sometimes end-over-end, as if they were chasing their tails. And maybe they were, it was kind of hard to tell.

It was a hazy morning, not very warm, and beside us on the shore about 85 seagulls kept up a constant bickering. Two ground squirrels came along and after a little hyperactive scampering, ended up on separate rocks facing the water, for all the world as though they were watching the sea otters with us. A woman with a leashed dog walked

by, prompting shrieks of irritation from the gulls
but no reaction at all from the otters. A man with a
styrofoam coffee cup stopped to watch for a minute.
Across the bay's mouth we saw a small flotilla of
pelicans land.

The otters lay on their backs in the water and
reached short front paws down to grab flippery back
fins and bring them up to their mouths. I imagine
they were licking them, although I didn't see any
sign of tongues. They scrubbed behind their ears.
Do sea otters have ears? When the front paws were
moving, there was a chain reaction, like the one
dogs have, and the back fins would also move, so it
looked as though they were dancing a little jig.

My friend Margot and I are not naturalists.
Walking down the beach, earlier, we couldn't
tell curlews from godwits, and when these otters
first came toward the shore with only their heads
showing, we mistook them for seals. The scene
wasn't even vaguely wild, either: there's a frontage
road ten feet away and the Morro Bay power plant
looming behind it. But here were these amazing
creatures, very blasé, right in front of us, six feet
from land, just living their own lives.

I wondered aloud why it makes me so cheerful
to see animals in the wild, and Margot said "It's

because they're straightforward. There's no hidden agenda." That's certainly part of it — a kind of simplicity and lack of guile. But what I also love is the intense paradoxical feeling that they are like me and at the same time nothing like me at all. I too wash my ears in the bath, although nowhere near this thoroughly.

The otters finished flapping and spinning, then settled on their backs among strands of kelp, heads resting between front paws, and fell asleep. This was a lovely sight, but after a few minutes somewhat boring.

In an effort to practice the straightforwardness of the natural world and not hide my agenda, I said to Margot, "Well, shall we go find some lunch?"

Frozen Charlottes

A few years ago, I went back east to visit my
cousins. I've been doing this since I was born, my
mother in San Francisco being very attached to
her sister, who lived in Ipswich, Massachusetts. We
visited every summer when I was a kid, ran wild in
the salt marshes, shucked an enormous amount of
corn for the 8 cousins and 4 parents in the family,
and slept soundly on screened-in porches in a pile,
like exhausted puppies.

But it's only been as an adult that I've learned
to go mucking. Isn't that a lovely word? Full of
onomatopoeia: the sound being like the action it
describes. Mucking is when you go out into the
Ipswich River at low tide, barefoot, right at a wide
corner below the South Street Bridge, and look for
treasure. The sound your foot makes coming out
of the slick mud is what I mean by onomatopoeia.
A slurping, sucking, wet-but-not-entirely-liquid

sound as your toes wiggle the mud out from between themselves and you pull on the convex shape of your arch.

Back in the day, which extended from 1750 to at least 1900, Ipswich residents threw their trash into the river. This was common behavior and not as bad as it sounds, since there was no plastic packaging then, and everyone composted. Paper or fabric wouldn't last a season, and wood was usually saved for burning. What mostly ended up in the river were glass, clay, and porcelain, and over time it all washed down to the ocean, the edges softened by water and mud, some things disappearing forever and some remaining only in shards.

This wide corner of the river captured a lot of the bits and pieces, and gives them back to us sometimes at low tide, especially after a storm. My cousins Michael and Donald are the mucking experts in the family: They've found perfume bottles intact, sometimes even with stoppers, the bowls of clay pipes, delicate hand-painted pieces of tea cups and saucers, colored glass, metal odds and ends, and even a few of the prized "Frozen Charlottes."

Charlotte, in the old folksong, was a girl who didn't follow her mother's advice, and left off her coat on the way to a ball so her party dress wouldn't

get wrinkled. She consequently froze to death.
Originally from a poem by Seba Smith, the tale's
been immortalized in the ballad "Young Charlotte,"
by William Carter. The dolls are teeny (1 to 4
inches) unglazed porcelain, and not jointed: They're
"frozen" into position, another reason for the name,
and were originally made as "Victorian bathing
dolls," for children to play with in the tub.

My cousins tell me they were also put in tea
cups to absorb the heat so you wouldn't burn your
mouth. Wikipedia says they were sometimes baked
into cakes for the birthday girl to find. Being only a
fair-weather historian, I don't really care what they
were for. That they existed at all and can be winkled
up through the mud with my bare toes centuries
later makes me incredibly happy.

The View from Here

It's been a while since I've had occasion to see
the human form, male version, naked, from behind.
Luckily, this circumstance was remedied over the
weekend, when I went to the coast to house-sit for
some friends who live in a little beach town. It's not
a nude beach, but it has decent surf, and therefore
attracts surfers. No, they are not nude surfers! Calm
down and let me finish the story...

This small beach town has a hill, with many
wooden cottages built every which way, cheek by jowl,
all with big banks of windows facing the ocean. I was
in one of those, still half-asleep, sipping my morning
coffee and watching the waves curl and break, when
a movement down on the street below caught my eye.
Caught my eye and then held it, while a muscular
young man standing next to his car took his pants off.
He then quickly wrapped his loins with an old brown
towel, but by that time it was too late, I was riveted.

He looked around furtively a couple of times,
but there was no one on the street. As he inched
into his wetsuit — feet, shins, knees, thighs — the
towel moved around in a compelling way, until he
had the suit almost up to his hips. Then — the
timing was perfect — the brown towel slid off onto
the pavement and most of his *gluteous maximi* were
again revealed.

I'm afraid, dear listener, I giggled. Men's butts
are a thing of beauty in general, but there's also
nothing funnier than watching someone try to be
discreet and fail, when you are the person they can't
see is watching. Also, our culture takes so much
pride in showing off women's body parts day in and
day out, it's refreshing to see something else for
once.

The *gluteous maximus* is the largest muscle of
the posterior and one of the strongest in the body.
I'm only telling you this to prolong the suspense.
I won't go into the make-up of rubber wet suits or
why the boards are short now instead of long: that
would just be mean. I will say that this street in
front of my friends' house is right above a short-
cut to the beach, and therefore the parking is free,
instead of $10 at the official parking lot. Ergo,
there's a parade of surfers' cars parked here from

dawn to dusk. And no one arrives already wearing
their wetsuit.

Poets are born observers, which came in handy
since seven more guys disrobed in front of me,
only one of them able to keep his sarong in place.
Sometimes they were alone and sometimes in pairs,
chatting away as their butts gleamed in the sunlight
and they grabbed at the falling towels. No one, alas,
turned completely around.

Last year, my friends put in a web cam so they
could see weather conditions while away from
home. They're thinking of adding another, aimed at
the street, and charging a subscription to internet
viewers.

This certainly cheered *me* up, far more than
those eagle-nest cams — I'd subscribe in a New York
minute. Plus, it's got to be good for your heart rate.

All Bets Are Off

Yesterday at my house it was 104 degrees on the outdoor thermometer.

In the shade.

We're in the middle of June, but only last week it was pretending to be winter, plummeting to 48 degrees, and I actually turned on the wall heater.

I like weather, I really do, but this is ridiculous. Wildly exaggerated melodramatic swings are not my favorite thing, in weather, romance, or any other part of life. I try to stay on an even keel now that I'm at the far end of middle age and my hormones have run off to Barbados without me. I've learned from cats there's very little worth getting too upset over, and what's unavoidably upsetting can usually be cured with a nap or a few canned sardines.

"On an even keel" is a sailing metaphor, meaning that your boat is right-side up and well-balanced: not tipping too far to port or starboard, not dunking the mast into the water which might cause you to turn completely over. We use it in speech kind of casually, but the meaning of the phrase is life-savingly important, and even as a metaphor, I take it seriously.

One way I've learned to get along in the world is to know what I must bear and be prepared for it. This includes taxes, emergency vet bills, unexpected tooth extractions, and heat waves. I was born into a San Francisco fog bank. My comfort zone ranges between 66 and 74 degrees Fahrenheit, with sunny skies and a cool breeze lurking offshore so you know not to panic.

When I moved to the Sierra foothills, it was in the mistaken belief that the weather here would be briskish, sort of like the mountains, not hellish, like the Central Valley, where three-digit temps are par for the course. I've made peace with my mistake, choosing not to move away yet, and it's been 20 years. The way I've learned to cope is to work up to the heat slowly, drinking gallons of extra water and talking myself through the high-80s and low-90s in a quiet voice over several weeks until I can function normally. If I start to feel a little desperate, I fling my body into a lake full of melted snow and concentrate on its beautiful turquoise color until I can calm down again.

However, 104 degrees is not in my contract, especially not when it pounces like this. The window air conditioner is still in the shed and there are winter coats hanging on the coat rack. Instead of writing, editing, or otherwise making a living, I've had to limit my expectations to folding laundry and watering plants. I can't even make a sandwich, it's too complicated: I just eat half a cucumber while driving back up to the lake. I've been swimming so much my toes don't unwrinkle during the hours I'm out of the water.

Now I hear Thursday's supposed to get up to 108. That's just absurd. If the whole summer is planning to behave this way, I'm telling you, all bets are off.

Folklore & Mythology

It is very very hot in our town. Over at my house, with the new wider road giving us more asphalt to absorb heat and the chopped-down trees no longer providing shade, it's running ten degrees hotter than the announced high for the area. Today it was 106. If you think I'm complaining, you have read me right. I am definitely complaining. And I'm probably going to keep complaining, because I have well-developed tenacity and stamina in this department.

However, since I was not born yesterday, I know complaining is fruitless. The gods of heat waves, climate change, and road-widening projects are turning, as usual, a deaf ear. If they exist at all. It rarely matters that my college major was Folklore & Mythology, but I have actually *studied* the way human populations create stories to explain the world to themselves and their children. Almost

all the stories include a larger force who could be
helpful but at the last minute is not. Make of that
what you will. I think it indicates in humans a deep
desire to be saved, even though we always end up
having to save ourselves and usually each other.

I'm saving myself with a small window air
conditioner next to my desk, and a large lake, 20
minutes away. I feel guilty about using electricity to
power the air conditioner, and gas to power the car
to get to the lake. This is First World, middle-class,
Baby Boomer guilt, with some coastal-California-
native thrown in. It's not usually so hot that coastal
Californians need air conditioning, so a measure of
disdain for the stuff has developed over time. This is
a mix of real concern for ecology and an egotistical
Boomer feeling that *we* must lead the way to
change. Sprinkle in nostalgia for a particular kind of
Western-pioneer suffering, and you have the perfect
formula for regional guilt. Plus my parents were
Yankees, so add a dash of righteous Puritanism and
there you have it: my psyche, in a heat wave.

Luckily, cooler heads prevail around here: I have
friends and mentors to turn to, who say, kindly,
"Turn on the a/c and go take a swim for God's sake,
before you lose your mind. And while you're at it,
try to accept the unacceptable." Have you heard this

horrible phrase before? I think it's originally a tenet of Buddhism that weaseled its way into the larger American culture, especially in California, where it admonishes us all for complaining.

I dislike being reprimanded, even gently, by ancient religions, but I see the point. By complaining, I waste my breath, a finite resource. Breath I could use to pull myself past the beautiful pines and maples on the shores of the lake. Breath for laughing at the goofy things my friends say while we're swimming.

If I stopped complaining, I might, in fact, be able to cheer up and not be quite so cranky even though it's 106 in the shade!

Harumph.

I'll think about it. I hate to let go of something when, through years of practice, I've gotten so exquisitely good at it.

Sharing

It's the ninth day our skies are thick with smoke,
and again my heart sinks. I get ready to feel angry
and demoralized because I'll have to stay indoors.
Then I remember that I have a house to stay inside,
and am grateful the fires are not burning *our* houses
down, they're a hundred and fifty miles away.

Gazing at the gray sky, watching shadows on
the sidewalk that look like we're in the middle of a
solar eclipse, for some reason makes me think about
sharing. I don't much want to breathe in particulate
matter, but it is a form of sharing the damage, of
being part of an event far away. More practically,
we're sending local fire fighters to Redding,
Mendocino County, and Yosemite — people from as
far away as Australia are fighting these fires. We've
driven supplies, food, and money to evacuation
centers, and even livestock trailers to help move
animals away from harm.

I'm sorry it takes a big disaster for people to break out of our habits, but I'm glad we do. Most humans have an impulse to help, to give, to shelter and protect others who are in trouble. If we have the resources, we share them.

In Northern California, three years ago, half the rural town of Weed burned to the ground and shocked us all. Last year it was big parts of Santa Rosa. Today it's Redding, a small city. The terrain around Clear Lake has burned all three years, and the mountains near Yosemite. We're sharing in the after-effects of these fires: a housing shortage, high prices for building materials, insurance rates soaring or policies cancelled. People with enough money are moving into my town, three hours from San Francisco, so things here are growing and changing. But there's no reason to think we'll be spared — our landscape is drought-stricken timber, too, and jerks are still throwing cigarette butts out their car windows into dry grass.

This year, after talking about being prepared to evacuate, a bunch of us actually got our go-bags ready, and they're by the door. Water, granola bars, cat carriers, small bills for vending machines. I don't remember where the nearest vending machine is nor what it contains, but in a bad fire who knows

what high school gym or Vet's Hall or Elks Club
we're going to end up in. We shared information on
what to put in the bags. We shared the urgency to do
it sooner rather than later.

As you know, other parts of the world are
flooding and freezing, blowing away in tornadoes,
covered with hot lava. I think for me what's
changing this summer is that somewhere in my
body, my animal body, it's registered that this is
going to continue getting worse and I'd better let
go of fond memories of cooler summers and snowy
winters. Last year this was a thought I was trying to
wrap my head around. Today, early August, mid-
morning, under smoky skies, it's in my cells. I'm
alert for the sound of fire planes overhead and which
direction they're going.

If there is a consolation, it's that we're here
together.

Be Joyful Though You Have Considered All the Facts

I went swimming today, as I often do, in a lake 20 minutes from my house. It's a human-made lake, not a true natural lake, which you can tell because there's a dam at one end they let water out of all summer, lowering the surface and therefore the boat dock by several feet each week. Now, in early September, a stretch of red dirt shows all along the edges and large tree stumps have been revealed on the shore. A little aspen took root a few years ago beside the dock, or rather, it's beside the dock when we start swimming in late May. Now it's half-way up the ramp. Being of a literary and a sentimental bent, I sometimes wonder, when I'm swimming back toward the dock, whether it misses its tree at this time of year. They are reunited a month after the rains begin, when the lake fills up again.

Yeah, I know, I'm a sap.

In one way I have the ideal swimming body:
I'm buoyant in the extreme. I'm also strong in the
shoulders, so even though there's a lot of me to
haul around, I eventually get where I'm going. At
this lake, I'm going to the left, toward what we call
the Santa Fe House because it's made of adobe. I
like to think the distance is a third of a mile from
dock to beach, so I can say I've swum two thirds of
a mile, but I don't really know. And I never actually
touch land. I would if it were sandy, but it's rocks
and soggy, slimy dirt, a.k.a mud. Everyone has their
phobias and mine is oookiness underfoot. So I swim
close to shore but stay over my head, and then turn
around and swim back. I don't sit on the bank to
rest, but sometimes I float on my back and look at
the clouds. Being buoyant, my feet come zooming
up from below me and I have a chance to admire the
fact that my toenail polish matches the lake. Then
my midsection rises and blocks out the sight of my
toes, and I sigh and think, "I wonder if I'll ever lose
any weight?" Then I think, "Who knows?!?" and
look at the clouds again. There's no point in ruining
a beautiful cool relaxing invigorating refreshing and
fabulous swim by thinking about your weight.

Today, I was alone. No friends came with me, no
motorboats were out. The two kayakers disappeared

in the other direction and the paddle boarder walked up the ramp to his car. I righted myself and twirled slowly to get a 360-degree view. It's a fine lake. When your face is that close to the water, it's a dark turquoise-teal color that makes me inordinately happy. Suddenly I though of Wendell Berry's great line: "Be joyful though you have considered all the facts."

"This is what it feels like to be happy," I said aloud.

"I'm still thinking of the wildfires and smoke, Houston's flood wreckage, the huge hurricane headed straight for Miami. I haven't forgotten South Asia's monsoons or melting polar ice. But right now, here, in this blue lake, nothing is wrong, and I'm lucky, and grateful, and wet, and happy."

I hope you can find your happiness, too.

The title is a line from Wendell Berry's "Manifesto"

Blackberry Picking

The other day I went to a local farm to pick blackberries. I have plenty of my own blackberries here at The Poem Farm, but they aren't ripe yet, and they're usually the size of a green pea, borne on arching stems that are so prickery you really should wear long sleeves to pick them. My friends run what used to be called a "truck" farm. They provide produce and fruit to local restaurants, the Saturday farmer's market, and many families in the area.

As I've reported before now, I'm a bad bet to have even a half share of a weekly produce box. I'll make a few salads and maybe a big veggie omelet but the rest of the stuff ends up in my compost pile, which is so wasteful I can hardly bear to admit it. So I buy at the farmer's market, and try to spend my dollars equally between all my farmer friends.

When you live by yourself, you get a lot of leeway in the food department. I've recently taught myself to eat three meals a day, and make sure I'm getting enough fruit and veggies. Although sometimes I still revert to a cheese and cracker dinner at my desk, it's pretty rare. But there's only one of me. A loaf of bread gets hard before I can finish it, and two heads of lettuce is plenty for a week. I don't actually need to buy much from the farmer's market.

But as the eldest of four, I was exposed four separate times to all the books in the Little House series by Laura Ingalls Wilder, read alternately by my mother and father in the living room after dinner. I've never gotten over the thrilling idea of putting things up for the winter. I'm also a big fan of inexpensive Xmas presents. Blackberry-merlot jam is this year's flavor.

Eight a.m. in a California summer is a very good time to be out in a berry patch, especially this one. My friends planted a thornless variety whose fruit is the size of my entire thumb. I think I picked six pounds of blackberries in 15 minutes, without ever having to sit on the ground and look up to find the ones that hide under leaves. And that doesn't include the 10 or 12 that I ate.

Earlier in the week a customer told my friends he'd picked berries as a job when he was young, and the boss made him whistle the entire time he

was working, to make sure he wasn't eating any. If
you're a boss, that's such a simple and effective idea!
And if you're a picker, how disappointing!

Yes, I paid for these, which I won't have to do
with my own berries. But they're so delicious I
couldn't resist. I went a little wild giving jam away
in July, but I use the smallest jars, so there are
lots of them. I got a jump on the Xmas season and
experienced one of the great pleasures of an old-
fashioned summer: acting just like a contented bear.

Ferris Wheel

When I was 14, I developed a short list of
requirements for being a good girlfriend. Heaven
knows where I got this idea, maybe from reading
Seventeen Magazine. You had to be able to gut a
fish and cook it. You had to be brave enough to go
skydiving (but only once per boyfriend).

In my long career as a girlfriend, I've only gutted
two fish and I have never gone skydiving. I can't fly
without Dramamine, so the idea of skydiving is just
silly. You might as well throw me out of the back
of the plane and be done with it. At 14, I was eager
to have a boyfriend but also a little scared, and I
poured my trepidation into the list. A big fear like
skydiving was easier to talk about than a big fear
like sex.

I don't know if other pubescent girls made lists
or not, but I think it's a feature of our culture for us
to feel there are some things we *ought* to do — that

are required of us. Some people need to have tidy
yards to keep up with the Joneses. Families with old
money seem to need to give lots of it to charity, while
families with new money don't. We even choose our
clothes using cultural cues we never think about.
If you saw me in baggy knee-length shorts with a
baseball cap on sideways you'd think I was ready for
Hallowe'en, but generations of kids have dressed
that way and no one blinks an eye.

One of the great things about middle age is how
the culture loosens its grip. Or maybe we've lived
long enough to value our own preferences more
than any outside standard. Which brings me to the
county fair, where I was last night, gazing fondly at
the ferris wheel.

I love the way ferris wheels look: that simple
shape, a circle, a wheel, so huge against the sky.
Its iconic stature as a symbol of summer and fun.
How it's a thrill but a mild one, not some loud, fast,
jerky, screaming ride. My impulse to get on the thing
is overwhelming, almost magnetic. I want to be a
happy American and sail above the earth in a little
bucket, looking down over treetops and Safeway's
parking lot like an eagle.

But I know better. Two years ago my sister
and 12-year-old niece convinced me to join them

on the ferris wheel and then got to watch me have a full-blown panic attack. I thought maybe things had changed but by the time we were five feet off the ground I was on the floor, my legs and arms wrapped tightly around the center pole and my eyes screwed shut, hyperventilating. They were laughing hysterically. After a while they figured out I wasn't kidding and then patted me occasionally on the head and described the view. I don't think my niece had ever seen a grown-up decompensate before, so she was kind of fascinated.

I'm just going to have to be a happy American on solid ground because getting airborne isn't my thing. Fish guts, maybe. Ferris wheels, nope. And skydiving? I must have been out of my mind.

Skydiving is for the birds.

Praying for Possums

I live a fairly quiet life in a rural area and don't often feel visceral fear. Near-miss traffic accidents will shoot my adrenaline through the roof, or smoke from a wildfire that looks close, but by and large my days are uneventful, just the way I like them. Two years ago when the first possum marched in my open kitchen door, I thought that was high drama, especially since it kept running under the sofa instead of back out the door. *Ha! Little* did I know.

This summer there are no possums. However, last night I was sitting at my computer by the kitchen door, writing a poem. It was hot, still in the low 90s, and the door was wide open onto my deck. Various cats walked in and out, but I didn't pay much attention. At some point, the chewing sound coming from the cat food bowls four feet away sounded unusual. Possums have trained me to listen for irregularity in chewing patterns, but this didn't seem as loud as a possum.

I looked over in that direction, and my face went white. My body stayed perfectly still, but I produced enough adrenaline to lift a Volkswagen bus over my head with one hand. It's a very strange sensation to have that much panic and electricity coursing through your body but not move a muscle. I took a few silent deep breaths and tried to relax my neck. Sid was pretending to be asleep on the desk, though I could tell he was watching. No other cats were in sight.

"My goodness," I said in a soothing voice. "You have a very fluffy tail, there!"

The skunk kept crunching his or her way through the first of two full bowls of Science Diet. "When is it," I asked rhetorically, "that skunks are most likely to spray?" Since I was already at the computer, and the skunk was clearly not leaving soon, I looked this up on Google, typing softly. Not that often, actually. Just when they are startled. Chomp, chomp. I let out my breath.

"*HIIISSSSSSSS!!*" My head whipped around, the skunk whipped around and raised its tail to full height. Jack had arrived and was not happy to see his food being devoured. The three of us remained poised and motionless for long enough that my neck froze up again, and then the skunk turned back to eating and Jack jumped up and joined us on the desk. "Holy F-word," I said out loud, but serenely. "Don't do that again!"

We sat there, quite still, for what seemed like a few weeks, until the skunk took its pointy nose and beautiful tail back outside, pausing at the water bowl for a drink. I waited as long as I could stand it — about 90 seconds after the drinking sounds had stopped — and then got up to close the door. And lock it.

12 hours later, I am not recovered. I could probably still lift a Mazda Miata over my head. The screen door's been ordered. The cat door is locked. Please join me in praying that there's never a next time.

IV

When Nobody's Looking

By the second week in January, most people have either broken their New Year's resolutions or are clinging to them the way a climber clings to the face of Half Dome just after her feet have slipped. This is not a pretty sight, and it's so unnecessary. I don't know why people torture themselves this way. The first day of 2007 was especially seductive because it fell on a Monday, the time-honored day for drinkers, smokers, and dieters across the land to start over.

Changing one's habits is best begun on a Thursday afternoon in March, if you ask me: when nobody's looking. You can still say "I haven't had a drink in 46 days." No one cares exactly when this happened, they'll just be proud of you. The Monday morning/New Year's Day phenomenon stems from erroneous thinking anyway, because it holds out the false hope that change happens all at once, when instead it occurs in fits and starts, with back-sliding a normal part of the deal. New Year's Day dangles the carrot of perfection in front of us. Too bad we're not mules.

What we are — according to *The Female Brain,* a book that's making the rounds — is Neanderthal. Human brains are so strictly designed for immediate survival and propagation of the species that most of modern *life* seems a little superfluous, much less New Year's resolutions.

Neanderthal wiring is responsible for the widespread failure of diets: eating less food, all of a sudden, makes our bodies react as if we were starving. *No Mastadon stew! Not even fried grubs!!* So it does what it was built to do: puts up with starvation until the famine ends — say at week three of the South Beach Diet — and then scarfs everything in sight.

It seems that Stone-Age wiring is also responsible for an amazing fact: female orgasm has only one correlative — that is, there's just one thing they've found that influences its frequency, and it's not how much you love your partner, his stupendous anatomy, or the size of your headache. It's how *symmetrical* he is, in face and body — symmetry having been shorthand for genetic health, back in the day, and female orgasm promoting successful impregnation. I don't think same-sex relationships were part of the study, since they don't propagate the species, but I bet it still applies. I bet it applies to everything, even the apples we choose from the produce bin.

Try that on for your next resolution: *I am determined to become more symmetrical! I know I can do it!* If this fact were widely known, we'd all be getting spam about male face lifts instead of about Viagra.

In terms of resolutions, I vote with the Twelve-Step crowd: one day at a time, starting this minute. Therefore, at lunch today, I'm going to eat more salad than usual, and afterward take a walk instead of a nap. What will happen tomorrow is anyone's guess.

Submission

Here it is, a cold Wednesday in January, and I did not win a prize. There are actually many days of the year — in fact most of them — when I do not win a prize, but this is one of the days when I'm standing at the mailbox, reading an apologetic letter telling me that I didn't win a *specific* prize. In this case, the promise wasn't money but book publication. The good news is, I was one of 30 finalists, out of a thousand entrants. The bad news is that they chose five books, none of them mine.

I like winning prizes a lot. I like the initial elation. I like telling my friends: hearing their delight and amazement. I like thinking fondly of the wonderful poem that won, which has suddenly become a very *good* poem even though last week I thought it might be verging on mediocre.

Once you've been a winner, you understand that they telephone to say you've won, they don't write letters. So just seeing the letter in the mailbox is a bad sign. Being a finalist is a good thing, never doubt it. But I've been a finalist quite a bit, and it can get demoralizing. Almost more demoralizing than *not* being one, because it gets your hopes up. And hope, as we all know, is a fickle mistress.

Like many people, one of the things I try to do — without turning into a Pollyanna — is see if there's anything I can learn from my experiences. Poetry has taught me a huge amount about life. Writing my first poems showed me that I wasn't afraid to do something new. Having them praised reminded me of my capableness: that I'm smart and aware: I can figure things out. Having them critiqued and learning to revise was one of the great lessons of my life, because it taught me — after the six months I spent resisting the idea — that no matter how good a poet I might *think* I am, I'm a) not perfect, and b) can get better.

The hardest lesson — the one that writers are taught over and over — is rejection. We write a poem or a book, we send it out, and it comes back. This particular manuscript has come back more than 20 times. It's like having your kid thrown out of every nursery school in town: very, *very* personal. It makes me feel frantic and unloved.

But rejection is a huge part of life. We don't get picked for the soccer team; we don't get jobs we want, or apartments we covet on Telegraph Hill, or the phone number of that cool-looking guy in the corduroy jacket at the Sweetwater. It's awful at the time, but it happens *all* the time. The trick is not to let it stop you.

So I'm going to walk up to the house, make a cup of tea, and take another look to see if there's anything I can improve on. Then I'll do what I tell my students to do: put the book in a fresh envelope, address it to another contest, and drive it down to the Post Office. You definitely can't win if you don't submit.

Just keep in mind that they don't call it submission for nothing.

Winning a Prize

Recently, I mentioned that I had *not* won a poetry prize. It seems only fair now to tell you that I *have* won a prize. It happened like this:

I was standing in the kitchen on a Monday morning around 7:30. The second cup of coffee was running through the filter and I was frizzling up the milk when the phone rang. At that hour, it's usually my friend Stevie. *Hello!* I said, the way you greet a friend. *Hello*, said a voice. *Is this Molly Fisk?* When people use my last name, it's mostly a bad sign, but this was too early for Dish Network. *It is*, I said, a little warily.

This is Kim Bridgport from the University of Fairfield, she said. Aha, I thought, could it be? I had spoken to Kim before Christmas, when she'd called to say my poem was a finalist for the Dogwood Prize, in Fairfield, CT. They wanted First North American Serial Rights to put it in the May issue.

Hey, Kim, I said, carefully putting down the cup
of hot milk and walking into my living room where
there's nothing breakable. *I'm delighted to inform
you*, she said — I started bouncing a little on the
balls of my feet — *that Marilyn Nelson, our judge*
— I let some of the bounce get into my knees — *has
chosen your poem "Washington Square — New York,
1941"* — Oh! The bounce came all the way up from
my knees and out my mouth — she paused — *for
this year's Dogwood Prize.*

Oh, thank you! I said, in a controlled tone, *this
is wonderful news! We're very happy*, she said, *when
the judge chooses one of our favorites.*

By this time I'd turned 42 shades of pink and
was silently walking around the room like a great
blue heron traversing hot coals. I'm not a person
who makes lots of noise, so I have to do something
else with excitement. I flapped one hand as if
trying to shake off a cobweb, and then switched
the phone to my opposite ear and flapped the other.
Kim mentioned W-9 forms and disbursement, but
I couldn't focus. I had to twirl around the room
with my kitten Angus in my arms. When his claws
revealed a strong preference for being put down, I
leaned against the front door and made faces like a
fish trying to say "Wow!" It was actually me trying

to say *Wow!* but I didn't want to interrupt Kim,
and I wasn't sure if the noise would be reasonably
decorous, worthy of a prize-winning poet, or if it
would be more like the sound a lioness makes when
she comes into heat.

Kim went on and on, bless her, and I hope I said
Mmmm, *I see*, and *Thank you so much*, in all the
right places. When she hung up, I tried a little cheer,
which sounded idiotic. I said *OH!* six times really
loudly. I told the cats the good news, and then went
to see if my face had changed in the mirror. Yes and
no. Same smile full of fillings, same overhanging
Norwegian eyelids, but a different light behind the
eyes — part happiness and part unholy glee.

I couldn't be still, so I picked up the phone and
walked out to the deck to pace up and down and call
all my friends, starting with Stevie.

Not Quite There

This morning I finished paying my monthly bills, which I do by hand in a coffee shop the old-fashioned way, and as I was driving home, got into a familiar argument with myself.

"Hey, great, the bills are done!" I said.

"Not so fast, Buttercup," said I. "You have to put them in the mailbox. Then the job will actually be over."

"Oh, piffle," I replied, which is a time-honored phrase in our family for when you disagree but have no decent argument to put forth. "They're totally finished! The Wonder Woman stamps are affixed, the little return name tags are on there, what's your problem?"

"Molly, the point of paying bills is that the money *arrives* at PG&E and your usurious credit card bank, not just that you write the checks and seal the envelopes."

"Oh, piffle," I said again. Then I sighed, changed lanes, took the Broad St. exit toward our town's post office, pulled into the parking lot, and dropped the sealed envelopes down into the gaping maw of the blue drive-by mailbox. Don't tell my other half, but I did indeed feel a teensy *soupçon* of relief as I let them go.

After a lot of research, it's my opinion that humans are different from each other. One example is the way we approach tasks. There are quick starters who peter out in the middle, good steady plodders, and people who can't get going but once in gear race to a blistering finish. I am a 7/8ths gal. I can start fine. I can continue cheerfully through most of the process. And then, seven-eighths of the way along, when the end is in sight and you can almost hear faint cheers from the grandstand, I completely abandon whatever it is and move on to the next thing. I'm not proud of this, but I've come to understand it's a consistent pattern.

My friend Margot, in Cambridge, used to swing by every couple of months and say, "I need something to do: What's under your bed?" I would groan as she dragged out the big box of unfinished projects. Over the course of several years, she knit the last sleeve on a woolly green sweater, bound the buttonholes on what ended up being one of my favorite dresses, and put the backing on a quilt I had made out of my mom's old Liberty blouses. She took some abandoned flannel and made me a wonderful nightgown. I was horribly embarrassed at the time, since back then I believed I had to be perfect. But I still let her help, and thereby learned a powerful lesson.

Nowadays, I know that if I can't get myself through that last eighth of a task, I need to find someone to hold my hand. None of us is good at everything. We all need help. The way to make life work smoothly is to find people who can do the thing you're hopeless at, and figure out what you can do for them.

Oh, what was my side of the bargain? Every now and then, I could say something silly enough to make Margot, a serious woman from central Maine, laugh until she cried.

You Got to Have Friends

The other day a man I know sat down next to me at the counter of my favorite coffee shop and said, "Molly, what is a friend?" I must have looked startled, because then he said, "Are we friends? I like seeing you here, but I'm not going to be inviting you to my house for dinner any time soon." This is why writers frequent coffee shops: sooner or later all the big questions of life come and find us there, it's inevitable.

This man – I was going to say "friend" but clearly that's up for debate – let's call him Emil – owns a local business, and I see him once every week or two. If he comes in for coffee with someone else, they sit together and we joke when I go past their table on my way out. But if he comes in alone, he often joins me at the back counter and we talk about all kinds of things: small businesses, the weather, our town's nutty demographics and economics, proposed shopping centers, which pillars of the community eat lunch where, you name it.

Most people, over time, develop radar about each other. You can tell who's dangerous and who's benign, who's sarcastic, or quiet, or can't keep a secret. Regarding Emil, my overall thought was "trustworthy." And I was right: last fall when I thought I was having a heart attack right there at the back counter, he was the one I mentioned it to, which resulted in my riding to our hospital's Emergency Room in a red truck full of spruce trees. In my book, this sort of person is called a friend, despite my not having been to his house for dinner.

However, I understand what he meant when he asked the question. For me, friends come in all guises, from high school bestie to college roommate to favorite checker at the IGA. I make friends with my poetry students and make students out of my friends. The delineations are porous and shift around, but make sense to me.

One of my friends isn't even a person, it's this radio station, KVMR. I love it for the music, the sexy and goofy broadcaster voices, the programs that make me think. Like a dental hygienist, a barista, or someone you banter with at a coffee shop's back counter, KVMR has never been to my house for dinner. But I listen to it so often in my kitchen it feels like we're old friends. And I rely on the reports of traffic accidents, weather, lost dogs, and wild fires. That's why I give my support during their pledge drives.

What do you call someone who isn't included in the central part of your life, but of whom you're fond, or just see regularly? "Close acquaintance" sounds like being damned for faint praise, and "distant friend" an oxymoron. Buddy? Cohort? Neighbor? Fellow American?

There isn't a good moniker for the relationship, even though these connections make up the fabric of our communities, not to mention a person like this might some day save your life.

Wild & Scenic

It's a gray morning, but with the promise of sun
by about noon. Not too many cars out at 7:30, no
school busses yet. The usual suspects, including me,
are at their usual tables in coffee shops looking at
phones or gazing out the window. You might think
this was an ordinary place if it didn't appear so often
on those *10 Best Small Towns to Live In* lists in
national magazines.

I grew up in a beautiful, sleepy San Francisco
suburb. By the time I got out of college, the cost
of living there had outpaced everyone my age, and
now it houses only millionaires and the very old
parents of my high school friends. Even from afar,
the stages are predictable: first, there's a wave
of people who move in from the city to give their
kids a more bucolic life. We were in that batch.
Hiking up on the mountain or walking downtown
to the movies was a lot more fun than nagging our

parents for rides in the City or God forbid taking
the bus.

Then traffic picks up, parking meters go in
downtown, and — my personal bellwether — the
hardware store either closes or moves to a mall
by the freeway. This is important. Or maybe it
isn't important any more, with the internet, but it
used to be important because it defined a place as
a working town. The minute your hardware store
moves out, you have a bedroom community full of
commuters or a tourist town, or both. Something
about being able to buy half-inch screws and get
a key made on your walk past the market and the
library is essential for real town status.

When I moved to this little burg in the foothills,
the parking meters were in and the hardware
store already gone. I didn't relocate to offer kids a
pastoral life, I just wanted one myself, and found an
uninhabitable fixer-upper I could fix up. There are
now five cafés and a brewery inside the city limits,
next to stores named Spirit House, Luxe Nomad,
and Inner Path.

The second signal of doom for a place remaining
affordable is when well-meaning residents get
together and start a film festival. After movie
stars found Mill Valley, the rest of us were toast.

We have a little more leeway here in Nevada City, despite having *two* film festivals, because the older, more famous one is environmental, so most of the people who descend on us — who will descend on us tomorrow, in fact, in their Patagonia jackets — have at least heard of the concept of sustainability.

I'm oversimplifying this to make a point: of course there are other factors, like cyclical population booms, airbnbs, and the Silicon Valley diaspora. Personally, I love both film festivals. But you can feel the change coming. More Teslas, more stores selling steam punk clothing, real estate going into overbid at already eye-popping prices.

I was startled but not surprised last month to see, parked on our main street at two in the afternoon, a bright blue Mazerati.

We're not in Kansas any more, Dorothy. Not you, not me, not even Toto.

Waking the Gnu

There's quite a lot going on in the world, you
may have noticed. Many people are now so quickly
connected to information that it feels a bit like
things from far away — false nuclear warnings and
late-night mudslides, for instance — are happening
directly to us. Human bodies respond to stimuli
whether it's real danger or just a depiction of
danger, which is why people scream at horror movies
despite being safe in their reclining seats.

In the studies of trauma recovery, one theory
is that acting more like a gnu can be beneficial.
Animals are often threatened in the wild, but seem
rarely to remain traumatized. When a lion, say,
grabs a gnu by the back of the neck and drags it
home, the gnu goes limp automatically, playing dead.

It might actually *be* dead, depending on the
initial bite, but often it isn't. Then, when the lion
drops it next to a pride that's too full from just

having eaten something else, and leaves it alone, the gnu gathers its courage, waits for the right moment, and springs up, running away to safety.

What's interesting is that after the gnu is out of danger, it begins to shake, an uncontrollable shaking, kind of like what we do when we get seriously too cold. This lasts a while, maybe 20 minutes, and then stops, and the gnu resumes its life of eating grass, making baby gnus, and racing across the veldt seemingly without a care in the world.

In my town we have no veldt, and the lions are elusive. But with all the social and anti-social media out there, I think we're getting traumatized on a daily basis and not really knowing what to do about it. Drinking more coffee doesn't seem to help, so we feel depressed or pick fights or swear off Twitter for the 47th time.

Maybe we need to do some purposeful, regular shaking. I'm trying it, anyway. In this currently crazy political climate I think it might help to get in touch with our inner gnu. You are welcome to shake anywhere, but I've been staying out of the public eye and using my living room. I set the kitchen timer for five minutes — like all exercise, you want to work up gradually to your target. Then I turn on some zippy music and commence to shake. It feels extremely weird and also kind of great, and five minutes later my head is clear, I'm usually laughing, and my days, thus far, are much less tense.

It's so hard to figure out how to be empathetic and helpful to others but still live inside our own lives. I find it a constant balancing act, accompanied often by strong emotions that leave me drained and unenthusiastic. The Inner Gnu Method — I'd better trademark that name even though the idea comes from Peter Levine and Ann Frederick's popular book *Waking the Tiger* — really does help.

If nothing else, you will giggle, which, as everyone ought to know by now, is the most potent kind of healing.

The Mistral

Oooh, baby, I woke up this morning on the wrong side of the bed, the house, the town, and the planet. I am cranky like you wouldn't believe. I did NOT go to my exercise class, I did NOT eat a healthy breakfast, and I am NOT sorry, either. I have a few deadlines, like writing this stupid essay, but otherwise I am supposed to be on vacation starting today, and I am crawling out of my skin for no reason.

Unless the reason IS the vacation, but that's just dumb. The other thing is, it could be the wind. Yesterday and all night long and right this minute we are having one of those winds you see in the movies: a mistral, the kind they have in Southern France. A Santa Ana by any other name. The sort of wind that drove pioneers crazy on the prairies, knocking over their Conestoga wagons and sending their mules, oxen, and cast iron frying pans flying.

I was okay yesterday: finishing up some tasks,
being brilliant on the telephone with my coaching
clients. When they're cranky, I know exactly what
to say! And I'm nice to them! When I'm cranky,
I look for the nearest rusty shovel with which to
bash myself over the head. See? I can even keep
fancy syntax together in this mood, I am THAT
AMAZING!!! But I probably shouldn't be driving,
although I was just at the grocery store. Luckily I
made it home intact.

If I had any hormones left I would blame this
mood immediately on them, but I am hormone-free.
I glanced over at a shelf at the store and spotted the
O.B. tampons, with whom I had a steady four-and-a-
half decade relationship, thinking to myself, "Wow, I
haven't thought about tampons in years!" Oh, how
quickly we forget.

I wish I could forget this dang crabbiness as
fast, it is really getting on my nerves. I want to run
away from home, even though I'm going on a road
trip next week with a friend. Next week is too far
away, and besides, today I don't have any friends,
I can't remember their names, and they probably
never really liked me anyway. If a tank of gas didn't
cost 60 effing dollars and I could find a bandana to
wrap my belongings in and a stick to hang them on,

I *would* run away from home. And YOU probably wouldn't even miss me, either. No one would notice my absence except five ungrateful cats, right around dinner time, when that familiar hiss and zing of the Friskies can being opened did not greet their furry cocked ears.

Wow, it is EXHAUSTING to be this cranky!!! I understand why two-year-olds fall asleep so fast right after they throw a fit. It's real work to keep up a head of steam like this, stay frustrated and bitchy, generally hate everyone around you, and feel simultaneously abandoned and put-upon. I might need to take a nap before I run away from home, even though it's only 10:00 in the morning.

And still, if you can believe it, windy.

Silver Lining

This morning at 7:00 I hopped in the car and drove up to the corner, made the usual right turn, and heard that ominous lump-a-dump-a-dump noise that is the hallmark of a very flat tire.

Oh, turkey fart, I muttered under my breath and got out to take a look. Yup. Very flat. I called Triple A and they said someone would be there in 70 minutes. 70 minutes is a weird amount of time, so as the operator, without irony, wished me a nice day, I thought about language and marketing. Has Triple A been yelled at for saying "your wait will be just over an hour"? Hours always sound longer than minutes, just like $3.99 sounds like 3 instead of what it is, which is 4.

By this time, several of those 70 minutes had elapsed and I got back in the car, which I had to stay with even though I can see the roof of my house from that corner.

A person could become very cranky about a flat tire, and I reserve that right in case it turns out I need to buy *four new* tires because I have all-wheel drive. I don't know when this nasty feature started, but it's one more way modern inventions make it hard to be poor. With all-wheel drive, your tires have to match perfectly in make and wear, so if one goes, the three good ones turn out to be useless. It still snows in my town, despite climate change, and we need all-wheel or four-wheel drive. Half my friends live on dirt roads you wouldn't want to get stuck on in any weather.

But for some reason I wasn't cranky, which is a small but significant miracle. I had not drunk any coffee, either. Cars where whizzing by and blowing my skirt around. The sun was cresting a row of pine trees and starting to get in my eyes. It took only 18 minutes for Brian and Mike to arrive in their huge tow truck. I'd never had a flat in this car before, so I didn't realize there was a brand new full-size spare under the back seat. The guys were quick and hilarious and I was sitting in a café drinking coffee barely half an hour later. I mean 30 minutes.

I also chronicled the whole thing on Instagram and Facebook to while away the time, so I got sympathy and camaraderie from people as far away as Watertown, Mass. and San Clemente, California. *Thank heavens*, I said to myself, *this didn't happen at noon, when it's supposed to be a hundred and two and you know the wait would have been 270 minutes. 7 a.m. really is the perfect time to get a flat tire.* Not to mention that this morning I had no idea what to say in my commentary for KVMR, and now, dear listener, as you have heard, I do.

The moral of this story is that even when you think the world is falling apart there are still a few things to be grateful for.

v

That We Are Helpless

How do I talk about fire when it's this bad
and there are so many, some with lines holding
them back and some uncontained, roaring through
neighborhoods and wineries, schoolyards, even
Trader Joe's? When my writing students get stuck, I
suggest they get more specific, focus on details.

On the map of our bigger of two local blazes,
the red part that indicates active fire behavior was
an eighth of an inch from the name of my road,
Newtown Rd., down at the end where it tees into
Bitney Springs, about five miles from my house.
Maps can be so comfortingly flat and you can fold
them up into thirds and put them back in the glove
compartment or just click "save."

As I was cutting my fingernails on Monday,
the first day of big fire, I forgot one. Spacing out
is a common sign of stress and distress, agitation,
anxiety, PTSD. I was so surprised to discover it,

brushing a lock of hair out of my eyes later, the scrape of one nail being longer. I am usually a fairly orderly person, symmetrical in my habits. Forgetting things used to scare me, but now I understand human nature better, and also have a lot more compassion, for myself as well as everyone else.

A friend just south of San Francisco was amazed that smoke from North Bay fires could be affecting her lungs, but it didn't surprise me at all. Smoke travels fast, and also can sit like a blanket, immovable, over our heads. It depends on the wind. Weather maps are showing that smoke from these fires has already reached San Diego and the Great Salt Lake, 750 miles away.

I can't watch the film of burning barns and subdivisions. In tragic situations, we have to balance helping others and taking care of ourselves. For me, visuals stay in my brain for years, so I avoid them. I'm also disturbed by newscaster voices, which fall into two categories at times like these: either more dramatic or more deadpan than usual. The nonchalance seems cold to me, and the melodrama hysterical. So I scroll fast through social media with the sound off, looking for charts of fire containment, lists of shelter numbers and needs that I can pass on.

Helplessness is always with us, but it's a reality and a feeling that human beings dislike. We will try very hard to avoid it, which is why conspiracy theories pop up at times like this: Who started the fires? How can we explain so much disaster and make sure it never happens again? Who can we blame? We want power to help and change and fix and stop and save. Being helpless feels like death.

It's good, if you can, to stop for a minute and take a deep breath. Soften your gaze and find something to look at or listen to, briefly, that is alive and well. Half a stick of butter on the counter. A colorful leaf against the gray sidewalk. Birdsong, radio rhythm and blues. The smooth surface of your gearshift, and — perhaps — symmetrical fingernails on the hand that holds it.

Avoiding Capitalism 101

Every now and then, I sit around the house
like a sloth and read mail-order catalogs. It's
really great. At this point, I have mostly bowed
out of popular culture and its sexy second-cousin,
advertising. I live far from billboards, have no TV,
only listen to public or community radio, get bored
with magazines, and long ago put an ad-blocker on
my computer. This is not out of high-mindedness,
particularly, just a sincere distaste at being told
what to do. I also need a lot of empty space in my
head so poems can germinate there.

But every now and then, as a person might
need to binge on horrible junk food like Twinkies
or Velveeta, my mind craves a break from the real
world. Sometimes it's Swedish mysteries, which I
can pretend are part of my writing research, and
sometimes it's catalogs, which I can't. They are
where you find out — even for size 3x — that saffron

is everywhere in women's clothing this fall and owls
are still trending in home décor. Saffron sweaters,
saffron skinny jeans, saffron lingerie. There are owl
vases, owl lamps, owls looking up at you from plates,
platters, and bowls...there are even owl towels, God
save us from the rhyme.

Owls and foxes arrived together on the retail
horizon, but I think foxes have not had the same
shelf-life. I could be wrong — boy, could I be
wrong — but this is my deduction after perusing
Viva Terra and *Uncommon Goods, West Elm,
Anthropologie*, plus *Crate & Barrel, Restoration
Hardware, Ulla Popken, Pottery Barn, Gudrun
Sjøden, Vermont Country Store, The Company Store*,
and *J. Jill*.

I am not, as I say too often, a wealthy woman.
But my upper-middle class background and an
impulsive dad with champagne taste taught me
awful habits. It's taken me years to learn not to
buy what I don't need. But I still like to sit on the
sofa every autumn, surrounded by glossy paper that
promises endless happiness and acceptance by my
peers. With a felt-tip pen I circle everything it would
be fun to own or give to friends. I dog-ear pages. I
throw out all my furniture, in my mind, repaint the
walls, and start anew. I take a lot of time choosing

colors and admire the snazzy backgrounds: rooms
full of good lighting with no Kleenex boxes in sight.

I don't keep this a secret, particularly, but I
don't think I've done it in front of other people,
either. It seems more a seasonal pleasure, like
egg nog, than a true addiction. It made me very
happy, a few years back, to discover my favorite
ex-boyfriend's mother did exactly the same thing.
We both filled out the order forms and added up
the totals, too, plus tax and shipping. On our
separate sofas, it turned out we were each spending
thousands. It was pretty funny.

And, like-minded to the end, after a few hours
we got up, mysteriously satisfied, and dumped the
entire armload of imagining into the recycling bin.

What You Can't Give Away

Yesterday I gave away a dress I bought in
high school. A long black dress covered with red
embroidery. A Bedouin wedding dress. I gave it to a
friend, so I'll get to see it again, and she is pleased
as punch. It was old when I bought it, and cost a
whole summer of saved wages at the folk art store
in Ghirardelli Square where I worked. I wore it on
dates, to concerts, to weddings even though it was
black. It's clearly "bohemian," but I hadn't heard of
that then, I thought of it as "folkloric." I hung out
with folk dancers and had red dancing boots that
matched it perfectly.

Big and tent-like on me at first, it somehow
became smaller as I aged. I've been hoping for about
20 years that I'd fit into it again, but even I can't
hold on to delusions this long, and it deserves to
cover a living body again, to feel a heartbeat under
that gorgeous heavy cross stitching.

People say we carry emotional weight from every possession — I don't know if that's true, but it sure felt good to clean out the godawful mess in my laundry room. The portable closet was wrecked from cats sitting on top and shredding the flimsy covering. Half the contents had faded right shoulders from sun damage over umpdeump years. Some of these we will try to dye or patch over, but some won't make it in their original form. One handy friend will use them as fabric for other projects. Another is going to cut off sleeves, so marred dresses turn into usable jumpers. I won't be doing any of this, thank heavens. My job was to let go and call the right people. I'll be sitting on the deck with my feet up reading a novel while all this productiveness is underway.

The portable closet was also helped in its demise by the weight of my mother's fur coat. You may have one of these, yourself. A lovely, useless object that you don't know what to do with. In my case it isn't mink, it's something called "mouton," popular in the 1940s, which means it was made out of a sheep. Given to Mom by her father-in-law when she joined the family. She wore it maybe 10 times before moving to San Francisco, where the weather and her not-very-high social status made it obsolete.

I wore it 10 times after she gave it to me, but it's been on a hanger since before many of you were born. And now, good grief! One fears spray paint from PETA and horrible insults when you even think of wearing fur in public. I agree with that argument in principle, but this is not a theoretical coat, it is right here in my house. I suppose I could make it into a cat bed, or give it to the local theater's costume department.

This seems to be a burgeoning problem for aging middle class Baby Boomers... our descendants, if we have any, don't want their great-grandmother's china settings for 12 or inherited fur coats.

Isn't that weird? Just another mystery...

Signs of Healing

Once upon a time, in a galaxy far, far away, I was a neat and tidy person. My shoes were lined up in a row in my closet, I wielded an iron like Betty Homemaker, all my kitchen cabinets were spotless, inside and out. I liked being this careful about my life. I was proud of a desk clear of papers and the underwear folded in color order in my top bureau drawer. And yes, I was somewhat scornful of other peoples' messes. What I didn't know at the time was that my compulsion to keep things neat stemmed from fear of consequences, not just a joy in beauty and order. It was a true compulsion: an act repeated outside the immediate control of the person doing it.

I was thinking of this today for two reasons. One is the rather large spiderweb being built in a light fixture over my kitchen sink — a sink that is half-full of dirty dishes from last Tuesday. I've been watching this web get bigger and more intricate for about a week, but still have not seen the spider. I'll probably wash the dishes this afternoon, and fold the clean laundry covering most of my sofa, too. I might even take a few science projects out of the ice box and reduce the funky smell in there. Then again, if I get working on a new poem, I might not look up from my notebook 'til way past dark.

The other reason I was thinking about my former neatnik self is that this month is dedicated to the prevention of domestic violence, something I know about from personal experience. I was addicted to order because I was trying to be good. I thought if I didn't make a mess then I wouldn't be picked out as a child who deserved punishment. In my case, the punishing was sexual abuse, which, now that I'm older, I know can't be stopped by any actions of a child. It's completely at the whim of the adults. But a kid can't afford to think her parents are bad, it's too terrifying. And developmentally, kids are self-centric. They see themselves as the origin of everything, all-powerful. So of course, they think they can stop the abuse. They try any trick, any magical combination of behaviors. If the abuse continues, they have no alternative but to think they themselves are bad for making it happen.

This is why domestic abuse takes so much time to recover from. It's not like the one-time trauma of a car accident or getting mugged on the street — it's not even like being kidnapped and raped. Being hurt by your family is so hard to fathom that it takes years to begin to unravel. And maybe you never completely get over it.

Me, I mark my healing by certain very personal landmarks, like dirty dishes in the sink, or an unmade bed. To the outside world these may look like signs of slovenliness or depression. But to me, they're victory flags. Every unswept floor, every eggplant fuzzy with mold in the back of the ice box is proof that I'm no longer afraid.

Women's Voices

Today is International Women's Day. The banks and the post office are open, though, so you may not have noticed. School is still in session, and I don't *think* it's purposefully to give mothers a break. Google sometimes acknowledges the day by making the two Os of its name the symbol for female, that circle with a cross underneath it. Few of my friends, female or male, have heard of International Women's Day, and I hadn't either, until I moved to Nevada City and turned on the radio.

A whole day of programming about women was remarkable, but more amazing than that was a whole day of radio without any men's voices. Sometimes it's not until you notice a thing's absence that you become aware of its presence. The basses and tenors were missing, and I suddenly realized how much airtime they normally had — not just on the radio — any radio — but in movies, on TV, on street corners, and inside my head.

This reminded me of that really annoying characteristic of dogs. Dogs get excitable, as I'm sure you know, and many of them jump on guests, run after squirrels, try to chew your favorite shoes, and generally wreak havoc. When you are a woman, and you say "no" to a dog, or "down," often nothing happens: you haven't gotten the dog's attention. But if you lower your voice and try to sound gruff and stern, as masculine as possible, the dog may look up from gnawing your suede pump. And if a man says "no" or "down" in a firm tone, quite often a dog will obey him.

I don't know if there's something more authoritative about lower voices, or if we're all just acculturated to them, living, as we do, in a world where men have more power than women. After so many centuries of men being the judges and lawyers and doctors and businessmen and senators and scientists and pianists and novelists, our brains are well-trained to link their deeper voices with knowledge, expertise, instruction, and the final word on any subject.

There are other social cues that make women (and dogs) pay attention to men — height and physical bulk among them — but I think the voice operates as a kind of short-hand for these: a lower voice equals more strength, and that has

implications. This works in reverse, too: a woman
with a particularly high, squeaky-sounding voice has
a very hard time being taken seriously.

On International Women's Day, hour after hour
of women talking, singing, crying, and laughing
on the radio worked some kind of magic on me. It
relaxed me in a mysterious way. And now, whenever
I hear Lucinda Williams or Madelaine Peyroux,
Anne Lamott, Kim Addonizio, Ani DiFranco, or
even Condoleeza Rice, whom I patently dislike, I feel
stronger. I'm not sure how to describe it. Maybe it's
the understanding of what it's taken each of them to
get to this point, to have this song or poem or speech
make it to the airwaves. How hard it is to lift those
sopranos and altos out of the low rumble of the
world so we can find out what they have to say, so
we can hear them.

In the sixties, feminists had a slogan: "Women
hold up half the sky." We should probably have
182-and-a-half days of the year designated as
International Women's Days. But we don't. We have
today, March 8th. I hope you'll celebrate with all the
women and men and girls and boys around you.

Thank you for listening.

The Cruelest Month

April, where we are right now, is National Poetry Month. I know, there's a month for everything from curing male pattern baldness to celebrating wooden teaspoons. I don't understand it either. Many months, if not all of them, shoulder multiple subjects without complaint. There are also National Weeks and National Days. National Poetry Day is not part of National Poetry Month, it falls in March, which is Women's History Month (containing, conveniently, International Women's Day). Someone had been drinking when they were making the calendar, I'm afraid. Would it have been so hard to move National Poetry Day up a few weeks so the poets of the world didn't get headaches trying to explain this to their millions of fans? March is also, I see from Wikipedia, Hexagonal Awareness Month. I am going to be *so* all over this next year, pointing out hexagons wherever I go, just you wait!

But I digress. It's April. Which I have always thought was kind of *my* month, even though I was born in July, because as well as National Poetry Month, it's National Child Abuse Prevention Month. My early poems were all about incest, and for a while there I was afraid I wouldn't be able to write about anything else. Luckily, after a few years, my subject matter expanded to dead whales, canoeing, bartenders, ex-boyfriends, you name it. And now, the sky's the limit! I've written about Mexican restaurant wall décor, hair salon products, sex in cars, and even national politics, which we won't go into here.

There doesn't seem to be a National Ex-Boyfriend Month, although September is National Honey Month as well as National Pain Awareness Month, which might suffice. You think I'm making this up, don't you? It's also Trucker Appreciation Month, if that's your bent.

Back to April. In April, since 1996, poets are expected to step up and be extra poetical, whatever that might mean. A black beret and sandals for some, a soapbox at the corner of Spring and South Pine for others. Perhaps reciting more poems at dinner parties, or just staring, like Wordsworth, at a "host of golden daffodils." This is after you "wander[ed] lonely as a cloud."

For me, a few more public readings, a local poetry festival, writing outside if it's not raining. My daffodils are more of a smattering than a host, but maybe I can squint and replicate the feeling of plenty. I'm becoming a little obsessed with memorizing poems as a way to keep my brain nimble in my later years, and of course when I have a new kick I tell everyone else they should be doing it too.

"April is the cruelest month," (T.S. Eliot) "breeding/lilacs out of the dead land, mixing/ memory and desire..." If you're a writer, write a poem. If you aren't, why not learn something by heart? Make sure it's a poem you love, because it will be there in your bloodstream for good.

You have just enough time to accomplish this before we all must straighten our spines and enter May, National Correct Posture Month.

Down to Zero

I'm sitting in a coffee shop as usual, wondering
what I might possibly have to say on the radio that
could do anyone any good or at least be entertaining.
The subjects of local driving habits and cat
indigestion have been thoroughly covered, although
on my way to town this morning someone did run
the West Broad St. stop sign. And Gracie, aged 17
and three quarters, weight four and a half pounds,
found the absolutely worst place to lose her lunch
yesterday, which was into, and then overflowing out
of, one of the pans surrounding a stove burner.

You know, where the little gizmo sticks out that
holds the flames? And there's a half-inch gap around
it that leads down into the bowels of the stove? I
am very well-acquainted with this area now, and it
is extremely clean. I will spare you the details, but
if any other person or animal were causing me this
much work I would divorce, unfriend, or take him/

her/it to the pound. Since it's Gracie, I just hold my nose and deal. Opinionated elderly felines who've been trying to sit on some part of my body for 17 years in a row deserve a little patience. She is clearly my Zen teacher.

I feel like crying, but not over Gracie's impending demise, it's because they're playing Joan Armatrading in this coffee shop, songs that meant a lot to me in my 20s. Before Joan was famous I used to walk home through Harvard Square and stop to listen to her. Quite a few dollar bills fluttered from my pocket into her guitar case. I loved her braided Caribbean/British-English voice. I thought she was insanely brave to stand there and not know if anyone would listen.

Now I *am* crying... Good grief. I wasn't a writer then, it would never have occurred to me to get up in front of people: I couldn't even tell stories at the dinner table. But there she was, day after day, wearing ordinary clothes and singing in front of the Brattle Theater or Design Research. Doorways where later we heard Tracy Chapman and ten years before had heard Bonnie Raitt.

I guess I'm crying because this is a brief musical recap of part of my youth, which is gone now. Music really does get into us and stir the pot. I can

see the great swathes of Marimekko fabric in the
DR window, and sun glinting off the plate glass
walls that were so surprising back then and are so
ordinary now. I don't live there any more, and most
of the people I loved who were part of my life then
have died.

There's nothing wrong with living in this town,
with its friendly coffee shops and disappearing
painted white letters attempting to spell out STOP. I
love people here, too.

But I want both. I want all of it at the same
time. I want everything to still be happening and
nothing and no one to ever be lost. And I can't have
that. It sucks.

All we get to keep is the music.

The Name of the Game

I'm sitting at my desk in the kitchen, watching a cat try to eat part of a cookie. Cats apparently don't have taste sensors for sweetness, and this is one of those cookies made of a layer of filling inside two crispy styrofoam rectangles with little squares on them. I can't figure out what the draw is, for the cat, without the sweetness. I don't think anyone likes eating plain styrofoam.

You know it's a slow day around here when I'm trying to parse the motivations of cats. A slow day for the cats, too, clearly. One could even wonder about the presence of the cookie, but it was a gift, in a package of many of its kind, that I am taste-testing and finding quite terrible.

It's so slow I've been doing odd-jobs around the house that have needed to be done for centuries, like finally pulling the rag rugs I washed off the railing. They were clean, I hung them out to dry, then it rained unexpectedly, then I had to leave them out much longer to dry, and then I forgot about them for a week or so, and now I've just spread them out on the floors where they belong. Any minute now a cat is going to throw up on this one here in the kitchen and I'll have to wash it all over again.

The problem is, two of my cats are quite old, and heading straight for the Rainbow Bridge, as those Waldorf students like to call it. They're siblings, one so thin I can feel every rib and vertebra when I pick her up. She still eats dinner, but then throws it up about every third time, after which I try to get her to swallow some egg or a little raw chicken, which she usually keeps down. She probably has intestinal cancer. My vet and I are trying to let her live out her life as comfortably as possible without drastic measures she would hate and I can't afford.

Her brother, the cookie-mangler, has started to fail at jumping on both my desk and the bathroom sink, so now he comes over and just claws me in the leg when he wants to get up on something that's too tall. He used to be substantial, and though I can't feel his ribs, he's probably lost five pounds this spring. When I swing him up onto my lap, I overdo it and the whole move turns into something one would invent to entertain a toddler. He looks pained, and I apologize.

Sometimes people ask me what it's like living alone. Believe me, I would tell them if I knew! There are six of us in this house, each with a digestive tract, strong desires, and different life spans. It's not the same as living with other humans, but it's absolutely not solitude.

Witnessing anyone on their way to the Rainbow Bridge takes some courage. Two at the same time is almost more than I can bear, especially these two, who have sat on parts of my body for hours every day for 18 years.

We don't have much choice, though. Bearing things is the name of the game we're in, pretty much. And love, which got us into this mess in the first place.

Be Mine

Mid-February is not the most cheerful time of
year. Usually the sky is grey and dumping torrents
of water on our heads or inch after cold, white,
accumulating inch of snow. The light is pale and the
ground is hard.

There's nothing much to look forward to, either,
because after February comes March, and no one
has ever liked March. The only bright spot on the
horizon — kind of a reddish, pinkish spot, with
a paper lace doily around it — is Valentine's Day.
Which is a mixed blessing, I grant you, having been
named for a Roman priest beheaded in the year
270 (who is now the patron saint of both affianced
couples and the plague) and focusing so heavy-
handedly on romantic, two-person, heterosexual
love.

I've been single on Valentine's Day, and had
to fight for my dignity. Even though it feels like

a frivolous holiday invented to sell chocolate and long-stemmed roses and revive the greeting card industry, the power of Valentine's Day to make even progressive, well-adjusted single people feel horrible is amazing. But despite the global advertising machine, the U.S. Banking system, and almost all political activity anywhere, *love*, not commerce, is what makes the world go round. So I vote for celebrating it, and for resisting the culture's idiocy at the same time. The way to do this is to not limit our appreciation to lovey-dovey love. Widen the scope, as my one of my ex-boyfriends liked to say, from the constraints of Disney-ized romantic love to include every sort of love.

You don't have to cut a heart out of construction paper, either: just whisper "I love you" to cousins and cockatiels, babies, turtles, ex-wives you resent, parents with dementia, strangers suffering in natural disasters, colleagues who talk too much and take credit for your work. Make February 14th the day you spill out love to the museum's coat-check girl, the assistant fire chief, the grocery store clerk, and the short-order cook. Close your eyes and beam some love even to people you normally hate.

Because the scents of chocolate and roses are strong aphrodisiacs, and Valentine's Day is also

about sex, send a little love to everyone you've
ever slept with, even if you don't remember all
their names. Celebrate what your sweet bodies did
together. While you're at it, send some praise "down
there" for heaven's sake! The culture misuses sexual
innuendo all year long to try to sell us cell phones,
cars, and time shares on the Gulf Coast. For one
day, let's be real and thank our excitable parts for
inspiring so much ink, as well as for bringing us
pleasure and heartache.

    Praise your nerve endings for always doing their
job, even in the middle of the night. Praise your
lower lip, the small of your back, your eye-lids. Go
on: you can do this. Praise the glorious hollow of
your clavicle and the winsome soles of your feet.

The Details

Yesterday morning, my photo was splashed on the front page of our local paper, which made me feel like a movie star. Middle-aged poets rarely get this feeling, and I milked it for as long as I could, e-mailing the link to my friends and relations and even showing my name in print to the cats. It's important to celebrate when good things happen. Heaven knows we get enough bad news these days! Five out of five looked up from their napping locations to see if there was food involved and then went back to sleep.

The article said I'd been teaching writing to cancer patients for 17 years. This is true. Cancer patients and their friends, caregivers, families, anyone involved. I've probably worked with 600 people all told, and most of them are still alive, which is a miracle and has nothing to do with my teaching skills.

The class helps people feel better in the moment, less isolated and alone, more a part of the human family. There's good scientific evidence to back up the benefits of writing as a way to boost your immune system. But I don't measure any of this. I ask my students to describe what they wore to the prom, the make of their favorite car, the view out their back door. We write about cancer, its humiliations, our sadness and rage. But also about the funny stuff: the ridiculous medical names, the weird things people say to make you feel better that make you feel worse instead. How many boxes of Kleenex or syringes of morphine one house can hold. Horrible hospital food.

We go more deeply into gratitude than you might imagine: revelations we've had, the incredible help from medical staff, all the wonderful people along the way. Getting so close to death and then living, at least for a little while, makes you thankful for the tiniest things: flavors and textures and melodies. Colors. I had half a grapefruit the day I got home after cancer surgery and nearly passed out in delight — I'll never forget the intensity of it.

The architect Mies van der Rohe famously said that God was in the details. Leaving God to more qualified people, I think life is in the details. In class, we just look for little snippets, sometimes profound but often frivolous, dredging them up from memory to re-examine. A lake we swam in, a dog we loved, rain in Mexico or Missouri, anything. Everything. Lawn statues. Lip gloss.

The thing is, if you aren't dead yet, from cancer or anything else, then you're still alive. This is somehow easy for the human brain to forget. Part of my work is to remind us all, myself included, that the details matter. They have made us who we are, and will be with us through to the end.

There's a line I love in a poem by Galway Kinnell called "Wait," that goes: "Distrust everything, if you have to. / But trust the hours. Haven't they / carried you everywhere up to now?"

Yes.

Yes, one at a time, one after another, they have.

Acknowledgements

Unlike my earlier essay books, funded by day jobs and loans from friends, *Naming Your Teeth* was made possible through the financial contributions of my patrons, both private and those on the arts-funding platform Patreon. I'm a long-time fan of crowd-sourcing for many reasons. It's egalitarian, it's a direct, immediate, and personal connection, and it's a great way to build and strengthen community. To be on the receiving end of this support means the world to me, and has boosted/deepened/expanded my creativity in all kinds of ways. I'm enormously grateful to my patrons, who include:

Pat Barrentine, Ruth Bavetta, Eileen Blodgett, Sue Brusseau, Nancy Jean Burns, Laura Cherry, Randy & Katie Chilton, Brion & Alice Dunbar, Joanie Ferenbach, Jan Haag, Eileen Hale, Judith Hill-Weld,

Sharon Hollis, Joanna Howard, Maxima Kahn, Julia
Kelliher, Debra Kiva, Marilyn Kriegel, Helen Lay,
Eugenia Leftwich, Robin Mallery, Talei Hoblitzell
Mistron, Anita Montero, Missy Patton, Charlotte
Peterson, John Schelling Pollock, Joanna Robinson,
Eileen Schmitz, Shannon Francis Schott, Nancy
Shanteau, Jinny St. Goar, Catherine Stifter, Deb
Stone, Heidi Vanderbilt, and many who prefer to be
anonymous.

About the Author

Molly Fisk is the author of the essay collections *Houston, We Have a Possum*; *Using Your Turn Signal Promotes World Peace;* and *Blow-Drying a Chicken*, and the poetry collections, *The More Difficult Beauty; Listening to Winter; Terrain* (co-author); and *Salt Water Poems*. Her essays have aired weekly as part of the News Hour of KVMR-FM Nevada City, CA since 2005.

Fisk is the inaugural Poet Laureate of Nevada County, California, and has been awarded grants by the National Endowment for the Arts, the California Arts Council, and the Corporation for Public Broadcasting. She works as a life coach in the Skills for Change tradition. Visit her at mollyfisk.com.

To order signed and inscribed copies of *Naming Your Teeth* or any of Molly's other books, please visit www.mollyfisk.com/writing. You're invited to join Molly's supporters on the arts-funding platform Patreon at www.patreon.com/MollyFisk

CPSIA information can be obtained
at www.ICGtesting.com
Printed in the USA
FSHW011125061218
54264FS

9 780989 495882